RAZIN LEWIS

The Quick History! United states of America

A fascinating journey in time crafted for busy people

Contents

Preface

In my book titled "The Quick History!" I have tried to capture the essence of a nation. The story of America is vast and diverse, making it quite a challenging task to encompass everything. It's like trying to contain the ocean's vastness in a bottle.

This book is designed for readers who want an overview of American history. It's for those who, amidst their lives, want to understand the picture without delving into all the details. It's for minds who seek a taste of history without feeling overwhelmed.

I am just someone with curiosity and respect for the past. While events, dates, and figures are undoubtedly important, I believe that it's the spirit of its people that shapes history. Their dreams, struggles, and resilience are the foundation of this nation.

This book represents my attempt to bring closer those stories that have influenced America. I hope it serves as a starting point for your explorations and reflections.

Before you start, feel free to Click Here and subscribe for free giveaways!

Thank you warmly, Razin Lewis

I

FOUNDATIONS

1

Indigenous Peoples and Cultures Before European Encounters (15,000 BCE–1491)

The First Americans: Origins and Cultural Diversity

Journeying Through the Ice Age: First Americans

Imagine North America approximately 17,000 years ago. Picture a land untouched by hands, where mammoths freely roamed icy landscapes and giant sloths lazily moved through ancient forests. In this world devoid of skyscrapers or bustling highways, the only sounds that filled the air were the gentle rustling of leaves, the calls of wild creatures echoing through the wilderness, and the crackling of ice. It is a forgotten realm lost to time. It serves as a captivating prologue to the tale we are about to embark upon – a tale that unravels the mysteries surrounding America's first inhabitants.

3

Illustration of a diverse landscape showcasing various Native American cultures

Who were these pioneering individuals who graced this varied land? How did they establish their presence in such an awe-inspiring territory? Let's take a trip back to the Pleistocene epoch, during its final stages, often referred to as the last Ice Age. Massive ice sheets covered a part of the northern hemisphere, and the world had a different look compared to what we see today. During this era, humans entered what would eventually become the United States of America.

Imagine a land bridge called Beringia, a stretch of land 1,000 miles long from north to south connecting Siberia and Alaska as we know them today. This bridge appeared due to the lowering of sea levels, which formed a pathway between continents. It is believed that groups of hunters and gatherers, our ancestors, crossed this bridge. However, their motivation wasn't to explore new territories; they were following their source of sustenance, tracking mammoths and bison across this harsh and frozen landscape. These early explorers may not have realized it at the time. They were partaking in one of the most significant migrations in human history. They laid the foundation for thousands of cultures with distinct languages and traditions that would thrive across the Americas. This period represented more than migration; it marked the birth of countless ways of life that would develop separately from those in other parts of the world.

Let's debunk a popular misconception: the migration to the Americas was not a single event or a one-time mass exodus across a land bridge. Recent archaeological discoveries and genetic research indicate that multiple waves of migration occurred, with people arriving at times from various locations and through diverse routes. Some might have traveled along the Pacific coastline using boats, while others may have journeyed through the interior as the ice sheets receded.

The Clovis people, named after the site in New Mexico where evidence of their culture was initially found, offer a glimpse into the lives of early Americans. Visualize a Clovis point—a crafted stone spearhead—and contemplate the skill and knowledge required to create such a tool, which played a crucial role in hunting large Pleistocene animals. It must be remembered that the Clovis culture represents one chapter in an extensive prehistoric narrative. Across continents and in far-flung regions, diverse groups flourished. Distinct cultures took root within forests, deserts, mountains, and coastlines; each adapted to their environments.

Civilizations Before Columbus: Diversity and Ingenuity of Indigenous Cultures

Let's consider another example of Cahokia—a city near present-day St. Louis. Around 1050 AD, this city was a center of culture and commerce, home to thousands of residents and impressive earthen mounds that still inspire wonder even today. Another example is the Hohokam people in the Southwest desert around 300 BCE. They engineered irrigation canals, transforming dry land into fertile soil for agriculture. These ancient civilizations were highly sophisticated. They had well-developed systems of governance, trade, agriculture, and art. They studied the stars, constructed structures, and crafted stories that explained their understanding of the universe.

As we explore these landscapes, it becomes clear that "prehistory" does not imply a lack of civilization but refers to a time before written records. The people during this period were far from primitive; they were problem solvers, artists, farmers, and astronomers. They embraced storytelling to pass down knowledge and legends through traditions.

Let's delve deeper into the world of these ancient cultures – unveiling a tapestry woven with innovation, spirituality, and resilience – challenging the simplistic narrative often associated with pre-Columbian history. Envision the Ancestral Puebloans in the Southwest, whose remarkable multi-story dwellings carved into cliffs showcase the skills possessed by early Americans. These structures, such as the Cliff Palace in Mesa Verde, were more than just dwellings. They served as strongholds, centers of worship, and vibrant communities—a testament to a society that knew how to adapt and thrive in an environment that could be both harsh and beautiful.

Their existence was not solely for survival. It encompassed purpose, meaning, and a profound connection to the land and sky. The Hopewell tradition, which flourished in the midwestern regions of the United States between 200 BCE and 500 CE, is widely recognized for its impressive earthworks and mounds. Some of these geometric shapes were meticulously aligned with lunar cycles, showcasing their profound knowledge of astronomy. Others served as burial sites adorned with artifacts crafted from mica, copper, and shells—a clear indication of extensive trade networks and a belief system that extended beyond death. Still, these societies also confronted challenges stemming from their reliance on the environment. The Mississippian culture succeeded the Hopewell. They faced significant societal disruptions around 1300 CE due to a decades-long prolonged drought. As fields withered under scorching conditions and rivers dwindled into trickles, this civilization, heavily dependent on maize (corn), suffered immense strain.

Maize held a role beyond being just a crop. It was deeply intertwined with the fabric of society, serving as a foundation and even having spiritual significance. When the climate shifted, it affected their crops and tugged at the very essence of their society. They had to adapt to these changes, transform their ways, or face disintegration.

These environmental challenges weren't unique to the Mississippians. The Ancestral Puebloans also experienced droughts that forced them to abandon their cliff dwellings and relocate. This served as a testament to the balance between these early societies and their environment. These relocations were more than movements; they were epic migrations where people carried the seeds of their culture, technology, and beliefs into new lands, planting them anew in unfamiliar soil.

In contrast, societies like the Haida and Tlingit in the Pacific Northwest took a unique path. Surrounded by forests and seas, they became skilled woodworkers and fishermen. Their stories were told through crafted totem poles that conveyed narratives through symbols and figures—each representing a chapter in a larger story of familial lineage, rights, and achievements.

People adapted to different environmental challenges in regions like the Great Basin and California. Resources were scattered here, leading communities to adopt mobile lifestyles with strategies for seasonal hunting, fishing, and gathering. They didn't build monuments or large-scale earthworks; their legacy was a way of life finely attuned to the natural rhythms of their surroundings. From the deserts of the Southwest to the lush forests of the Pacific Northwest, the earliest inhabitants of America were not just passive residents but active participants in shaping their environments. They practiced controlled burning techniques to manage forests and enhance hunting grounds, constructed fish weirs and irrigation systems, and engaged in early agriculture that eventually gave rise to some of today's staple foods.

The profound impact left by these cultures is not just a relic from the past; it is an ongoing narrative that continues to influence our modern world. Let's consider the Three Sisters: maize, beans, and squash. These vital crops in Indigenous agriculture were more than food sources; they represented a sophisticated agricultural technology. Native American tribes like the Iroquois and other Eastern Woodlands peoples planted them with an understanding that they would mutually benefit one another—a support system mirroring their societies.

Meanwhile, in the civilizations further south—such as the Maya, Aztecs, and Inca—remarkable advancements were taking place in fields like mathematics, astronomy, and engineering that could rival or even surpass contemporary European achievements.

Pre-Columbian America

Now, let's take a moment to step back and revisit pre-Columbian America with its vibrant mosaic. What can we learn from these societies? Firstly, it is incorrect to view the "New World" as a wilderness; it was instead filled with interconnected cities, villages, and trade routes shaped by active management by its inhabitants.

Secondly, these societies challenge any notion that Indigenous peoples are homogeneous. The diversity in culture, language, and society was immense. From the cliff dwellings of the Puebloans to the democracy of the Iroquois Confederacy, the first Americans were pioneers and peacemakers, stargazers, artists, farmers, and builders of cities. Their stories showcase the resilience and adaptability of humanity. They serve as a reminder that history's not just a sequence of events but a continuous tapestry woven with every breath taken, every path walked, and every tale told throughout time. These narratives deserve more than footnotes; they are essential chapters in the grand story of humankind.

As we bring this chapter to a close, let us remember history is not about an 'other' but about all of us—every individual playing their part in a complex, beautiful, tragic, and triumphant human saga. The Indigenous peoples of the Americas have always been a thread in this narrative—their significance cannot be overlooked.

As we bid farewell to civilizations like that of the Mississippian mound builders, Hohokam canal engineers, Puebloan architects, and countless others who shaped their worlds under the circumstances, we must now embrace a new dawn. This dawn will illuminate a vastly transformed world molded by encounters, conquests, and unimaginable change.

Religion and Spirituality Among Indigenous Cultures

Embarking on a journey to explore the spiritual realms of Indigenous societies, we will discover the deep connections between their beliefs, the natural world, and communal existence.

Conceive a world where every aspect of nature – the sun, the wind, the Earth – carries profound spiritual meaning. In a world where ancestral spirits guide your path, rituals and tales link you to the sky, land, and waters. This extraordinary realm, overflowing with symbols and brimming with presence, was a tangible reality for the Indigenous peoples of the Americas. Their spiritual convictions were not fragments of life; instead, they formed an integral fabric that united their communities. Religion and spirituality saturated every facet of Indigenous life, influencing everything from changes to significant rites of passage. Nevertheless, it is essential to clarify that there isn't a single, monolithic Indigenous religion.

The spiritual practices and beliefs of the First Americans were just as diverse as their languages and cultures. Look at the Great Plains peoples, such as the Lakota Sioux. They were known for their buffalo hunting skills and nomadic lifestyle, and their spirituality focused on the interconnectedness of all living beings. The Lakota had ceremonies like the Sundance, which were intricate rituals involving personal sacrifices for the community's well-being. These ceremonies served to renew the bond between humanity and the spiritual realm. The buffalo held a place in Lakota culture; it was not just a source of sustenance but also considered a sacred presence representing life and abundance.

On the other hand, in far Southwest regions, we find Pueblo peoples like Hopi and Zuni, who had a deep symbiotic relationship with their arid land. Their religious practices centered around kachinas, benevolent spirit beings believed to reside in mountain peaks surrounding their territory. Kachinas were supposed to bring rain and fertility, crucial for the Pueblo's corn-based agriculture. Community events featuring masked dances filled with symbolism honored these spirits and sought their blessings.

Now, let's travel across the continent to the woodlands of the Northeast, where the Iroquois (Haudenosaunee) flourished. The Iroquois believed in a spiritual realm that coexisted alongside the human world. Their matrilineal society traced lineage through the mother's side, and women held significant power, especially in decisions about their land and resources. At the core of their belief system was the Great Law of Peace, which constituted a constitution promoting unity among the groups within the Iroquois Confederacy. This law held both spiritual significance as it was believed to have been ordained by the Great Peacemaker—a prophet who brought together the Iroquois people during times of great turmoil.

While there were variations in practices among these cultures, one common thread ran through Indigenous religions: a deep connection between the spiritual realm and nature. This connection was not passive; it required rituals, respect, and an understanding that taking from nature necessitated giving back in return. This reciprocity served as a form of communication with the realm—an ongoing dialogue between what can be seen and what remains unseen between humanity and divinity.

Indigenous Peoples Deep Connection to the Environment

One aspect that often captivates our imagination but remains inadequately understood is the relationship between communities and their surroundings. Standing mountains, tall prairies stretching, expansive intricate waterways, and dense forests were not mere backdrops for Indigenous people's lives; they actively participated in their cultures, economies, spiritual beliefs, and social structures. Then, seeking relation with nature, they embraced a stewardship philosophy and reciprocity– values that modern societies are slowly coming to appreciate in these times of environmental crisis.

A portrait of a member of the Lakota tribe stands, gazing at a herd of buffalo in the distance.

Just picture a world where each stream, stone, and breeze carries its story, holds spiritual significance, and has a shared responsibility within the community. This isn't the "wild frontier" people often imagine when they think of pre-Columbian America. Instead, it's a landscape filled with relationships and responsibilities where humans are just one part of a complex, interconnected web of life. The concept of "Seven Generations" stewardship, embraced by the Haudenosaunee (Iroquois) people, exemplifies this philosophy remarkably. It encourages decisions with the well-being of seven generations into the future in mind – a contrast to the short-sightedness often seen in modern planning.

The Indigenous communities of the Great Plains, like the Lakota and Blackfeet tribes, provide another example. The buffalo (bison) played a role in their way of life – providing food, materials for clothing, and shelter, as well as holding spiritual significance. Yet they hunted sustainably. They utilized every part of the animal while understanding the delicate balance between necessity and preservation. They recognized that taking more than necessary would disrupt the equilibrium that sustained them.

In the American Southwest, ancient societies like the Ancestral Puebloans (formerly known as Anasazi) developed civilizations in arid environments through innovations like irrigation systems and drought-resistant crops. These advancements enabled them to thrive despite conditions.

The Hopi, Zuni, and other descendants continue to uphold these customs, demonstrating the long-term viability of their practices. In the Pacific Northwest, Indigenous communities maintained forest ecosystems through controlled burns, ensuring a landscape's vitality with valuable resources. In return, this land provided cedar for construction purposes, totem poles, and salmon—a staple food source harvested with deep respect for the fish life cycles.

These practices were not solely driven by necessity; they originated from a belief system emphasizing all living beings' interdependence. Chief Seattle, a leader from the Suquamish and Duwamish tribes in what is now Washington State, eloquently captured this perspective with his renowned quote, "The Earth does not belong to us; we belong to the Earth".

As we conclude this section, it is essential to reflect on how America's lands and waters have a history and to acknowledge the Indigenous peoples' profound and sacred connections with their surroundings. Their philosophies, shaped over thousands of years through learned respect and mutual exchange, provide a glimpse into a harmonious past and offer a potential path forward as we navigate together toward an uncertain future for our shared environment.

With a foundation laid and echoes from ancient times still resonating in our ears, we prepare to step into a new era. One filled with encounters, conflicts, and mergers that will profoundly shape the course of what would eventually be known as the United States of America.

2

European Encounters and Indigenous Responses (1492–1620)

Initial Encounters and Indigenous Responses 1492–1607

An era exploring the first meetings between Indigenous peoples and Europeans

Transitioning from earlier to more recent history brings us to a period of immense change, where profound interactions forever altered the paths of both Atlantic societies. Just imagine the astonishment, confusion, and sheer disbelief that must have overwhelmed those involved in these contacts. It wasn't a clash between two groups but the beginning of a series of events that would reshape history.

Imagined painting of The First Landing Europeans in America

In 1492, Christopher Columbus, an explorer supported by Spanish monarchs, embarked on a perilous trip across the vast and unpredictable Atlantic Ocean filled with mysteries waiting to be unraveled. Columbus's motivations were driven by desires for wealth, trade routes, and an ambition to spread Christianity. However, just like explorers who came after him, Columbus did not discover the edges of Asia as he had expected. Instead, he stumbled upon a "New World" already ancient and teeming with life.

This is where our story takes a turn. Let's delve into the people and the inhabitants of the islands that Columbus first encountered in what we now know as the Caribbean. The Taino society was intricate with established trade networks, agricultural systems, and spiritual beliefs. Their world revolved around the seasons, cycles, sea resources, and the communal rhythms of life that had sustained them for centuries. Nonetheless, their peaceful existence was about to be disrupted.

Columbus's arrival brought forth a whirlwind of change. What started as amazement soon turned into exploitation. In the eyes of the Taino, they were either seen as potential converts to Christianity or forced laborers. The notion of 'discovery' varied depending on one's perspective; to the people, it felt more like an invasion than a meeting of two worlds.

What did these initial encounters mean from an Indigenous perspective? While much has been lost over time, oral histories and archaeological evidence provide glimpses into a mix of curiosity and apprehension.

The Taino people and other Indigenous communities who encountered Europeans were not observers in their own stories. They actively engaged with the newcomers, negotiating, resisting, adapting, and forming alliances. Each community had its response to these meetings, reflecting the diversity of their cultures.

Let's consider the tale of Hatuey, a chief of the Taino people. Recognizing the danger posed by the Spanish, he fled Hispaniola. He sought refuge in Cuba and warned his Indigenous peoples about the violence and enslavement that followed these strangers from distant lands. Hatuey's courageous resistance against the Spanish was one of the recorded acts of Indigenous opposition. Rather than merely accepting changes forced upon them, he actively fought to protect his people's way of life. Sadly, his rebellion was short-lived, as he was captured and executed. Forever becoming a symbol of resistance and an emblematic figure during this era of 'discovery.'

In this web of early encounters between cultures, we also encounter La Malinche (or Malintzin), an enigmatic figure from Mexicos Gulf Coast belonging to the Nahua community. She was given as a gift to Hernán Cortés, the conquistador, and played a pivotal role as an interpreter, advisor, and mediator between different groups. La Malinche's story is complex; some label her a traitor, while others see her as a survivor.

Her remarkable ability to navigate the waters of conflicting civilizations was genuinely extraordinary. However, her story also sheds light on the challenges that many Indigenous peoples faced during this time—a delicate balance between survival and subjugation, between adapting to new realities and fiercely resisting the erosion of their worlds.

As we delve deeper into this era of initial contacts, it is crucial to remember that these contacts were far from uniform. Whether it was the people in the Caribbean islands or the diverse tribes across North America, each meeting possessed unique characteristics shaped by specific circumstances and individuals involved. These tales of contacts set the stage for centuries to come—defined by conflict, adaptation, and unwavering resilience.

This history chapter is often portrayed with oversimplified narratives, yet reality is anything but straightforward. It unfolded as a gripping drama filled with ambitions, fears, misunderstandings, and an indomitable human spirit that has shaped our shared history.

Interactions influence societies and cultures.

The stories of our encounters with new cultures and environments continue to unfold, revealing tales of ambition, resilience, and unimaginable transformations. As we navigate these experiences, we encounter individual stories and witness the broader societal and environmental changes triggered by these first contacts.

The impact of these contacts was profound and diverse. Historians call it the 'Columbian Exchange,' which involved exchanging people and animals, plants, cultures, ideas, and, unfortunately, diseases. From a perspective, the 'New World' presented a land rich in resources ready for exploitation. They introduced crops like wheat and sugar and animals like horses, forever altering indigenous and American lifestyles. On the other hand, Europeans were introduced to tobacco, potatoes, and tomatoes – products that would significantly shape their societies and economies.

This exchange was imbalanced in ways, especially regarding biology. The Indigenous peoples had no resistance to diseases from the Old World, such as smallpox, influenza, or measles. These illnesses spread rapidly through communities like wildfire in a dry forest – causing immense devastation. The demographic collapse was staggering; some communities lost up to 90% of their population. These statistics go beyond numbers; they represent real people, families, and entire cultures that were permanently changed. Alongside this catastrophe, the landscapes of the Americas were also transforming. With the decrease in population, once cultivated fields reverted to forests, animal populations once hunted by Indigenous communities thrived. These environmental changes had an impact on the remaining societies as well as the European settlers.

But in this era of shifts, Indigenous peoples were not just passive victims; they actively shaped their destinies by adapting to the new circumstances forced upon them. They embraced tools, engaged in trade, took advantage of European rivalries for their benefit, and even formed unique and diverse communities through intermarriage.

One fascinating story is that of Pocahontas – a name closely associated with the Jamestown settlement but whose true history goes far beyond popular myths. As a Powhatan woman, Pocahontas's life beautifully illustrates the interactions between Indigenous communities and English settlers. While her story is often romanticized, her journey – including her conversion to Christianity, marriage to John Rolfe, and travels to England – showcases how individuals navigated these intersections with nuance. Her life was characterized by mediation and adaptation; she embodied both the potential for understanding. She symbolized the profound changes sweeping across her world.

As we reflect on the lives of these individuals, we gain an understanding of the wide range of human experiences during this transformative period. The initial encounters between Europeans and the Indigenous peoples of the Americas were not footnotes in history; they were significant chapters in the human story. These interactions set in motion changes that reverberated through the centuries for better and worse.

Yet it makes us wonder: what thoughts occupied the minds of those individuals when they first caught sight of the unfamiliar sails on the horizon? What discussions unfolded within their communities as they grappled with the realities posed by these formidable strangers who carried remarkable objects and destructive instruments? It is crucial never to let the aspect of history brimming with its hopes, fears, and instinct for survival be overshadowed by a grand narrative focused solely on exploration and conquest.

Indigenous and the immense changes brought about.

History is like an endless tapestry woven with countless individual lives. As we explore the threads of early Indigenous European interactions, we uncover personal narratives that shed light on the strength, adaptability, and unwavering human spirit.

One such thread is the story of Squanto, also known as Tisquantum. He belonged to the Patuxet tribe, and his life story reads like a captivating novel filled with adventure, tragedy, and pivotal roles in history. In 1614, Squanto was captured by an English sea captain. Taken to England, he learned English — an invaluable skill that would shape his place in the annals of history. Upon returning to his homeland in 1619, he discovered his village devastated by diseases introduced by settlers.

Squanto's journey did not end there. One year later, the Mayflower pilgrims established their colony in Plymouth, dangerously close to where Squantos Patuxet village once stood. Here, Squanto took on the role of mediator and guide, teaching the settlers how to grow corn and fostering relations with the Wampanoag Confederation. His invaluable assistance is believed to have supported the colony during its most vulnerable years.

Squantos's story is a testament to human resilience, showcasing the ability to navigate between different worlds and exploring the complex legacy left behind by those early settlers. But it also raises thought-provoking questions. What motivated him to help those who, knowingly or unknowingly, had caused devastation to his people? What strength did it take him to forge a path toward peace in a landscape overshadowed by personal loss?

As the sun dipped below the horizon, casting a twilight hue over the Plymouth settlement, one can't help but wonder if Squanto stood at the shore with his eyes tracing the vast ocean that once swallowed him whole and spat him back into a forever-transformed world. What thoughts consumed his mind? Was it regret? Longing? Hope?. Perhaps an intricate patchwork of emotions as complex as the era he found himself in.

This era was not only defined by these encounters but also shaped by ripple effects that would resonate for centuries to come. Throughout history, the Indigenous peoples struggled to preserve their cultural heritage, lands, and political independence despite expanding European empires. A compelling example is the Haudenosaunee Confederacy, an alliance of six nations in northeastern North America. They had a system of governance called the Great Law of Peace, which emphasized unity and collective decision-making – a stark contrast to Europe's monarchical and often oppressive rule. During this period, the Confederacy demonstrated diplomatic finesse by engaging in trade and negotiations with Europeans while safeguarding their sovereignty. As we conclude this chapter, it is crucial to view these stories not as isolated events but as moments in humanity's voyage. The echoes of these encounters resonate throughout history like a symphony composed of triumphs, tragedies, hope, and resilience.

The Days of Colonization and the Relationship between Indigenous People and Europeans 1607–1620

Early colonization

As the sun rises in 1607, a new chapter unfolds in America's captivating story. Three ships, namely the Susan Constant, Godspeed, and Discovery, gracefully sail through the brackish waters of Chesapeake Bay. On board are men who mission to establish Jamestown, an English settlement that would become a fixture in the Americas. This monumental event is one piece of a giant puzzle called "Early Colonization and Indigenous-Europeans Relations", an era filled with ambition, challenges, and inevitable transformation.

Illustration of Jamestown, Virginia, during its early years

Our tale begins in Jamestown, Virginia, where survival was a gamble for these settlers. Picture this: air saturated with Virginia's summer humidity enveloping a group of pioneers who find themselves far from their familiar England. They are surrounded by wilderness, teaming with life unknown to their European sensibilities.

Under the guidance of the Virginia Company, the English ventured to this 'New World' in search of wealth, enticed by tales of gold and a shorter route to Asia. However, they were ill-prepared for the realities that awaited them.

The early years of settlement were plagued by starvation, disease, and tensions with the Powhatan Confederacy. Fortunately, the Indigenous peoples provided knowledge essential for the settlers' survival. Jamestown might have suffered a fate similar to Roanoke's without their assistance. Here, we again encounter Pocahontas, the daughter of the Powhatan leader. She becomes a symbol of hope amidst struggle as she marries John Rolfe in 1614—an act that could be seen as a choice driven by love or a maneuver. This union represented a potential for peace between two cultures, yet history reminds us that such moments of harmony are often fleeting.

Meanwhile, north, another colonial endeavor was taking shape. The Pilgrims—religious separatists seeking freedom from the Church of England—arrived aboard the Mayflower in 1620 and settled in Massachusetts. Unlike the primarily male settlers of the Virginia Company, the Pilgrims included families who aimed to establish a society deeply rooted in the land they had found. The first winter endured by the Pilgrims is a testament to their resilience against nature's unforgiving icy grip.

Many of them perished, their hopes and aspirations buried in the ground. But when spring arrived, bringing its message of rebirth, a new opportunity for alliance emerged. This is where we reencounter Squanto, a Patuxet man who had traversed worlds serving as a bridge between cultures. He imparted skills to the Pilgrims, including planting corn, fishing, and foraging. With his guidance, the settlers established a treaty with Massasoit, the leader of the Wampanoag people—a pact that would ensure decades of peace.

These initial years of colonization were like a collage, with faces—both Indigenous and European—each person playing an essential role in this mosaic-like society. There were moments of unity when the Pilgrims and Wampanoag shared meals in celebrations that inspired Thanksgiving. Despite that, shadows loomed on the horizon as conflicts threatened to undermine this coexistence.

Growing connections between Indigenous peoples and Europeans

As we delve into the 17th century, it's crucial to understand that the initial encounters between Indigenous peoples and Europeans were not isolated events but rather a more extensive web of interactions that would shape the fate of the continents. While there were instances of cooperation and peaceful coexistence, there was also a rooted sense of misunderstanding and distrust.

In what would become New England, European aspirations for expansion cast a shadow over the lives of Indigenous peoples. Initially extending gestures of peace, the Pilgrims were soon followed by other English settlers, many of whom did not share their commitment to harmony. The Puritans, who established the Massachusetts Bay Colony in 1630, were not merely willing to adapt to their new surroundings. Instead, they aimed to reshape it according to their society's ideals.

Picture the green forests teeming with a symphony of life and then gradually witness the encroachment of organized agriculture, fences, and farmland. For the Indigenous communities, this wasn't a change in the physical environment but a complete redefinition of their entire world. Land held a deeper meaning for them than being a mere commodity. It was seen as a sacred relative deserving of utmost reverence. This difference in perspective led to conflicts that escalated into wars spanning American landscapes.

Nevertheless, some individuals sought understanding and mutual respect amidst this mounting tension. Consider Roger Williams as an example. He was a Puritan minister whose progressive ideas were ahead of his time. Banished for his beliefs, Williams established Providence Plantations in 1636, which later became part of Rhode Island. He respected the sovereignty of Indigenous peoples by advocating for fair interactions and even tried to learn their languages. His writings offer insights into the Narragansett and Wampanoag cultures, acting as rare bridges of empathy during an era characterized by growing divisions.

Unfortunately, Williams stood out as an exception in an era dominated by practices of territorial encroachment. The Pequot War (1636- 1638) in present-day Connecticut marked a turning point. The conflict from trade competition with the Dutch eventually impacted the Pequot tribe. One horrifying example is the Mystic massacre, where English forces and their Narragansett and Mohegan allies set ablaze a Pequot village. These events may seem distant in time. They are an integral part of America's intricate history. They remind us that our nation's story is composed of moments of triumph and marked by profound tragedy.

We find ourselves on the verge of change as we delve deeper into this period. The dynamics established during the years of colonization were about to transform, paving the way for a new chapter in this ongoing narrative.

Key transformations

As the 17th century ended, a complex chronicle of American history unfolded, filled with cooperation and conflict. The diverse people who shaped this history faced challenges such as ambitions, cultural misunderstandings, and the relentless expansion of colonies.

Let us take a moment to explore the world of the Iroquois Confederacy, also known as the Haudenosaunee. This powerful alliance comprised the Mohawk, Oneida, Onondaga, Cayuga, and Seneca nations. Even before contact, they thrived through a sophisticated system of governance outlined in the Great Law of Peace. A constitution that brought these nations together. Their society valued well-being and operated with democratic principles that were quite remarkable.

As European settlements expanded across their territories, the Haudenosaunee found themselves precarious. They faced pressure from competing French, British, and Dutch interests from all directions. Despite these challenges, they navigated through diplomacy and strategic alliances. Nevertheless, the introduction of weapons and pressures brought about by the fur trade transformed intertribal dynamics and warfare.

II

COLONIAL ERA AND PATH TO INDEPENDENCE

3

The Complexities of Colonial Life
(1620–1753)

Colonial Communities: Interactions with Indigenous Peoples, African Communities, and Other Minorities 1620–1675

Early colonial America

As we step onto the cobblestone streets of colonial America, we are greeted with a saga of human experiences, a whirlwind of lives merging from distant corners of the world. By 1620, English colonies had already been established, and we were amid their growth and challenges. We are at a crossroads where different worlds meet and intertwine in intricate harmony. These days of what will eventually become a vast nation, we discover the origins of America's complex identity.

Imagine a town square where the atmosphere hums with a mix of languages, each voice carrying tales from faraway lands. Here, an Indigenous individual trades furs with a settler, symbolizing the connection between different worlds. In another scenario, a person, possibly a free individual or one of the first to endure the horrors of pervasive chattel slavery, negotiates over the price of tobacco. These ordinary scenes are the foundation upon which American society is built.

Illustration capturing the bustling atmosphere of a colonial town square in 1620

Let's zoom out and examine the larger picture. How did this diverse group of individuals come together on this stage? The story is filled with challenges and cruelty. It also shines with moments of resilience and unity.

The Indigenous peoples, who were originally the inhabitants of this land, experienced upheaval due to European arrival. From the Eastern Woodlands to the Southwest, these varied communities were no strangers to change. Their histories, cultures, and spiritual beliefs were rich and diverse. However, when European settlers arrived, it marked the beginning of an era defined by disruption.

For example, the Wampanoag played a role in supporting the early Pilgrim's survival. Squanto's assistance was particularly noteworthy; he was a Patuxet man who had endured kidnapping and slavery in Europe but offered guidance to help settlers navigate the terrain and establish crucial diplomatic relationships. Nevertheless, these early interactions were not without their tensions. The exchange was filled with tension characterized by a lack of trust and occasional conflicts, setting the stage for the relationships unfolding over centuries.

At the time, the transatlantic slave trade was beginning its sinister journey. This dark voyage resulted in millions of Africans being forcibly taken from their homes and subjected to unimaginable horrors. In 1619, the first known Africans reached British North America, their status unclear but precariously straddling the lines between servitude and enslavement. Their situation resembled impoverished Europeans who traded years of labor for passage to the New World. Yet, within a decade, this system transformed into the brutal institution of perpetual and hereditary slavery, leaving a lasting mark on humanity's conscience.

Amidst these changes, other minority groups sought to establish themselves in colonial society. Jews fleeing European persecution initially found refuge in cities like New Amsterdam, later renamed New York by the English in 1664. Dutch, French, and German settlers formed communities in areas and contributed their customs to the growing cultural mosaic.

As these diverse lives intertwined, colonial America became a mosaic of life's moments marked by shared struggles and profound divisions. During this period, a foundation was laid for developing a society undergoing continuous changes. This served as the basis for both the achievements and challenges that were to follow.

Colonial communities and their interactions

To truly comprehend the reality of colonial America, imagine walking through a dense, unexplored forest. With each step you take, new landscapes unfold before your eyes while paths intersect in ways. This analogy mirrors the lives and destinies of individuals and groups who contributed to shaping what would eventually become the United States.

Let's shift our focus to women in colonial America – unrecognized heroes of their time. Across all communities, women were pillars of families and local economies. In cultures, specifically, women frequently took charge of agricultural activities, community governance, and preservation of cultural traditions.

European women who settled in the New World played a role in ensuring the survival of their families and communities even though the patriarchal norms of their society often limited them. Similarly, African women brought forcefully to this land displayed remarkable resilience despite exploitation, maintaining family ties, and preserving cultural traditions against all odds.

Yet, these communities did not exist in isolation. Their stories were intertwined with a mix of cooperation and conflict. Let's look at Metacomet, also known as King Philip to the English. He inherited his father's position as sachem. He played a significant role among the Wampanoag people. His father, Massasoit, was instrumental in establishing peace with the Pilgrims. Nonetheless, tensions escalated during Metacomet's leadership due to disputes over land, resources, and cultural misunderstandings. Eventually, this led to the King Philip War in 1675—a conflict between the Wampanoag tribe and English settlers. This war marked a turning point that dramatically changed power dynamics in colonial America while bringing forth increased hostilities and land dispossession for peoples.

Amidst this period of societal transformation, African communities faced unique challenges and hardships. The shift from servitude to racial slavery did not happen suddenly, but during the mid-17th century, laws solidified the notion that Africans and their descendants were considered property. This dehumanizing treatment marked a departure from how European indentured servants were treated and established a racial hierarchy that would have long-lasting effects on the nation. Despite these conditions, African culture survived and assimilated into broader American culture through music, cuisine, and language.

At the time, various minority groups contributed to early American society's vibrant cultural, religious, and economic evolution. For instance, Sephardic Jews fleeing from the Portuguese Inquisitions brought distinct traditions and expertise in trade networks. German immigrants introduced techniques and architectural styles that have left enduring imprints on American culture.

This world was filled with contradictions and disparities where shared experiences coexisted with divisions. As paths crossed and lives intertwined, these complex interactions wove a narrative that was anything but simple yet held lessons still relevant today.

Colonial interactions and their lasting effects

In the landscape of colonial America, various paths continued to intersect unexpectedly. As we delve deeper into the half of the 17th century, it becomes clear that the destinies of Native peoples, Africans, Europeans, and other marginalized groups were intricately intertwined. This created a collage filled with diversity and marked by challenges and conflicts.

We must contemplate what defines a community. Is it merely a group of people residing in one place? Does it hold a deeper meaning? In America, 'community' was an intricate concept. It extended beyond coexistence; it involved adaptation, clashes, blending cultures, and, most importantly, survival. It revolved around the tales shared by African mothers with their children under the moonlit sky, the quiet prayers of Puritans seeking religious freedom, the solemn gatherings of Indigenous tribes that resonated in the forests, and the hopeful conversations spoken in various languages by other minority groups who dreamed of a brighter future.

In contrast, amidst this struggle for survival and self-identity, conflict often accompanies them. Following King Philip's War, the situation for communities became increasingly precarious. The war, although a desperate and courageous stand by the Wampanoag people, had consequences. It resulted not only in the loss of life but also in the loss of land, autonomy, and cultural heritage for Indigenous peoples. The advancing presence of settlers and factors such as the spread of European diseases further marginalized the original inhabitants. A narrative of conquest that cast a shadow over the nation's progress.

As for Africans in America during the 17th century, it was a time filled with sorrow. From the mid to late 17th century, laws and societal norms gradually shifted, solidifying a system of racialized slavery that emphasized racial hierarchy and exploitation. These laws stripped away freedom and identity, treating individuals as property and devaluing human life. The impact went beyond suffering and had profound psychological effects throughout the centuries.

In the most challenging times, there were signs of resistance and hope. Indigenous peoples and Africans found ways to resist oppression through rebellions, preserving their cultural heritage, or simply enduring it all. Their ability to bounce back is a testament to the human spirit, an essential element of American identity.

Furthermore, minority groups shaped the colonies' cultural, social, and economic landscape. They brought trades, skills, beliefs, and traditions that added depth to colonial life. Understanding these influences is crucial in comprehending the United States as it exists today—a nation whose identity is diverse.

As we conclude our exploration of America, remember this: history extends far beyond events and dates found in textbooks; it encompasses the real-life experiences of individuals and communities. It's a mosaic comprised of dreams, struggles, and interconnected stories throughout time. While challenges and conflicts mark some aspects of America's tapestry, they are integral to the narrative of a nation constantly evolving and redefining itself.

Colonial Administration and Political Assemblies 1676–1753

The emergence of administration and the political assemblies

As the 17th to the 18th century transitioned, it became evident that the American colonies were far from uniform. Each colony had unique laws, economies, and social customs under their respective European power's influence. During this period, we witnessed a transformation from vulnerable outposts of the Old World to distinct societies with their governance systems. This raised a question: How does one govern a new world using old rules? Who has a say in these matters?

An illustration of a diverse group of colonials gathered to discuss the growing discontent and the concept of

As we embark on this exploration, let's begin with an analogy: Picture a patchwork quilt. Each patch represents a colony, distinguished by its fabric and design. All these patches are interwoven by necessities, ambition, and humanity's unquenchable thirst for governance.

One of the regions, Virginia, is considered the birthplace of what many regard as the semblance of American representative governance. In 1619, the House of Burgesses began as a gathering where certain men discussed and made decisions on matters. It wasn't akin to democracy but marked a significant beginning—a foundational stitch in that larger odyssey.

Furthermore, let's not overlook the significance of Bacon's Rebellion in 1676, an uprising that laid deep divisions within colonial society. Think of Nathaniel Bacon, a dissatisfied planter whose ambitions matched the vast expanses of unsettled lands he desired. Bacon grew frustrated with what he perceived as Governor William Berkeley's neglectful attitude towards settler concerns, particularly regarding defense against Native American attacks on frontier settlements. This led to a revolt involving frontier settlers, including many indentured servants and enslaved individuals who rallied behind Bacon's promises of land and representation.

While the Rebellion and Bacon's life were short-lived due to his death from dysentery, their reverberations extended beyond colonial shores and resonated back to England. It revealed the dangerous consequences of popular uprisings and the volatile combination of a frontier society divided by wealth, land, and power. Bacon's Rebellion served as a precursor to the simmering tensions that persisted within and among the colonies, ultimately leading to the Revolutionary War.

As we move northward on our trip through history, we encounter a contrast in Massachusetts. Here, Puritan influence permeated every aspect of life, including governance. The Massachusetts Bay Colony operated under a rule where church and state were intertwined, and legal statutes drew guidance from biblical scripture. Although this system was rigid and sometimes harsh, it provided stability. It fostered a sense of shared purpose necessary for survival in New England's unforgiving climate.

There were dissenters within this framework, like Roger Williams. He espoused the idea of separating church and state and was exiled for his beliefs. He went on to establish Rhode Island as a sanctuary for freedom and dissenting voices—a rebellious addition to our ever-evolving history.

Throughout the colonies—from Pennsylvania, with its Quaker tolerance and commitment to principles to New York's diverse proprietary colony—each contributed its unique design to the fabric of governance.

Evolution of political structures

During the 18th century, the colonies experienced a phase of growth and transformation, much like adolescents finding their own identities. However, this era was not about identity; it was a time of political exploration and experimentation.

Let's shift our focus to the Middle Colonies for a moment. Imagine a mosaic where various European influences converged, giving rise to a society that stood out from the typical uniformity associated with New England Puritans or the Anglicized elite of the South. In this center of early America, diversity wasn't merely present; it was embraced and celebrated.

For instance, let's consider Pennsylvania as an example. Founded by William Penn as a sanctuary for his Quakers, it evolved into something much more significant: an experiment promoting religious acceptance and representative government. Penn's Frame of Government, established in 1682, guaranteed freedom of conscience and allowed the colony's landowners to elect representatives to a provincial assembly. This was groundbreaking for its time! Penn's "Holy Experiment" in Pennsylvania stood out starkly against the prevailing theocracies and rigid class systems elsewhere.

New York and New Jersey, with their blend of Dutch, English, and various other cultures, also contributed to this atmosphere of inclusivity. While still subject to control, they developed governing systems that granted a certain degree of self-rule that was considered progressive during that era. For instance, establishing an assembly in New York in 1683 following England's "Glorious Revolution" marked a significant shift. Its existence represented a move towards participatory politics that would later shape American democracy.

As we delve into these evolving structures, we must also consider the individuals they govern. It is important to remember that the narrative surrounding governance is not solely about laws, revolutions, or assemblies. It revolves around the lives impacted by these political systems, from the wealthy landowner residing in his grand estate to the humble craftsman working in his workshop, from the resilient indigenous tribes to the enslaved Africans on plantations.

Consider the consequences of laws like the Navigation Acts, which limited trade exclusively to British ships and ports. Suppose you are a merchant in bustling cities like Boston or Charleston, where your livelihoods depend on the decisions of distant lawmakers. Reflect on how property laws shaped who could vote, own land, and accumulate wealth, often excluding women, nonwhite individuals, and those without property.

In the colonies, an economic model based on plantation systems thrived, heavily relying on slave labor. The governance in these regions had to uphold and sustain this system, resulting in slave codes and laws that regulated chattel slavery. These laws impacted not only enslaved people but every level of colonial society.

As these colonial assemblies took root and expanded over time, they gradually began pushing against the limitations imposed by imperial rule. Sometimes subtly and at other times more forcefully. By the mid-18th century, these pushes had intensified significantly. Set the stage for a political confrontation with far-reaching implications.

Let's not get too ahead of ourselves. Before we continue, let's take a moment to pause and reflect. If you were a resident in these colonies, who would you be? Would you be a farmer struggling to have your voice heard? Perhaps a wealthy merchant trying to navigate the complexities of trade laws? Maybe an indigenous person fighting to protect your ancestral lands? What about an enslaved individual forging connections of solidarity and resistance?

Escalating conflicts that foreshadow the Revolution

As we delve deeper into the tapestry of colonial America, we witness the growing interconnectedness between governance, society, and individual experiences. Picture yourself as an assembly member during the early 1700s, whether in Virginia's lush rolling hills or Massachusett's rugged rocky coasts. Your position holds influence but is also riddled with challenges.

The colonies thrived as centers of commerce, culture, and

disagreements. Let us take this moment to step into your shoes as we dive further into this era. Finding a balance between the needs and interests of different groups within your community is always challenging. Whether they are landowners, humble farmers, or urban tradespeople, it's important to consider everyone's perspective while also considering the demands from the distant Crown across the ocean. Dealing with the Navigation Acts, which we discussed earlier, can be pretty frustrating, along with regulations and obligations imposed by a government thousands of miles away.

Now, as someone serving in an assembly position during the mid-18th century, you notice a shift in attitudes. Discussions among your colleagues, whispers in taverns, and debates are happening in town squares. The word "liberty" is gaining momentum. It is shared like a secret code that unites different factions under a common cause.

What has led to this growing discontent? It's a combination of difficulties caused by British trade restrictions, the lack of representation in the distant English Parliament, and an emerging sense of American identity distinct from its British counterpart. This identity is formed by a mix of people from various cultures and backgrounds within the colonies – it's like a stew that has been simmering for some time and is almost ready to be served.

What about those who are not directly involved in these po-litical circles? What about people, enslaved Africans, women, and those who do not own property? Their voices also need to be acknowledged and considered. Their stories, often overlooked in accounts, hold equal importance. For example, the indigenous tribes faced challenges as their ancestral lands were encroached upon by expanding colonies. Relationships between natives and settlers varied from trade and military alliances to conflicts and heartbreaking displacement.

On the other hand, enslaved Africans and African Americans found ways to establish pockets of independence amidst unimaginable hardships. They upheld their traditions and formed communities despite being subjected to forced labor that fueled the colonial economy – a paradox at the core of a society increasingly fixated on freedom.

In society, women played crucial roles in managing households, running businesses, or working on farms. While legal rights were limited for women, their contributions were indispensable to the colonial way of life.

As we approach the events of the Revolution, these intricate dynamics intertwine. The concept of liberty – cherished by colonists – becomes worth fighting for. Questions arise: Whose liberty is it? What does it signify for individuals within the colonies?

Guess the tension in the air before a storm – palpable anticipation. Visualize assembly halls filled with enthusiasm, bustling taverns, vibrant village greens, and bustling households. Feelings of dissatisfaction are ideas that were once considered extreme and are now being discussed seriously. The situation is reaching a boiling point, and the world, to most people involved, is on the verge of a permanent transformation.

As we conclude this section, let us remember the individuals who shaped colonial America. The assemblyman passionately argued against taxation, the native leader strategized to protect his community, the enslaved mother passed down songs of hope during dark times, and the woman managed her household while quietly contemplating her thoughts on freedom. Their stories intertwine to create an intricate narrative that weaves through history.

Religious diversity

The diverse religious landscape of colonial America and its profound effects on society

If we consider the developments in America as distant thunder, the religious passion that prevailed was like an electrifying charge in the air unseen but palpable before a storm. Our exploration of diversity in colonial America goes beyond mere beliefs; it delves into the stories of communities and sacred places amidst untamed wilderness conflicts fueled by strong convictions and even the quiet revolutions within individuals.

Picture a map of the colonies. Envision each region illuminated by its radiance representing prevalent faiths. These vibrant shades not only color the land but also permeate every aspect of life, including homes, governance, education, and the pulse of these colonies.

Painting of enslaved Africans recounting stories. In the distance, an Indigenous tribe holds a spiritual cerer

Our first destination is New England, where the Puritans' strict theocracy casts a blue-gray light. Their faith is characterized by precision and a belief in predestination. They seek to purify the Church of England and their own lives. The phrase "city upon a hill" represents more than a metaphor to them. It is a covenant with God, symbolizing their commitment to righteousness in a world they perceive as tainted by sin. Their way of life revolves around adherence to religious practices, blurring the boundaries between secular and biblical law.

However, the Puritan community is not without challenges and dissent. Some question the established norms; Roger Williams advocates for the separation of church and state and is subsequently banished. He goes on to show Rhode Island as a sanctuary for freedom. Anne Hutchinson, a profoundly devoted woman, hosts religious gatherings in her home where she challenges conventional beliefs and gender roles. As a result, she faces charges of heresy. She is also expelled from her community.

Moving southward to the Middle Colonies, we encounter a diverse religious landscape reminiscent of the varied colors of Joseph's biblical coat. Here, we find Quakers who espouse light doctrine advocating equality and nonviolence. Pennsylvania is a testament to religious tolerance under William Penn's leadership, attracting people from diverse backgrounds, including Quakers, Catholics, Jews, and Protestants from different denominations.

In the southernmost colonies, Anglicanism was prevalent as the established church of the English Crown. In this region, we can find pockets of other faiths, such as Baptists, Presbyterians, and a growing population of enslaved Africans who blend their traditional beliefs with the teachings of Christianity passed on by their masters.

But let's not view this diversity as mere background scenery in colonial life; it plays a significant role in shaping society. The churches, synagogues, and community gatherings are vital societal pillars beyond worship alone. They provide opportunities for education, social interactions, and even political discussions. Political dissent finds ground within these spaces amidst whispered conversations after sermons or lively debates during communal meals.

Yet vibrant this religious landscape may be, it is not without conflicts. Tensions often arise between denominations; accusations of heresy and fears of witchcraft result in trials and executions – most notably remembered in Salem. The treatment of people by various religious groups varies from attempts at conversion to outright hostility and violence.

Faith

As the colonies developed, the relationship between religion and politics also evolved. The religious enthusiasm that swept through the colonies transformed individual beliefs and ignited a collective consciousness. The ability to question, choose, and embrace one's spiritual path was not just about religious ideals but also political ideals.

Consider stepping into a Boston coffeehouse in 1765. It is a hub of ideas where passionate debates are occurring regarding the recently imposed Stamp Act. Among the patrons is Mercy Otis Warren, a woman known for her sharp wit and respected for her active participation in political discussions, even in male-dominated spaces. One can hear echoes of the Great Awakenings principles in her conversations—the emphasis on conscience and the challenge to authority. For Warren and others like her, the idea of equality naturally led to political equality and rights considerations.

It is important to note that this blending of fervor with political convictions did not mean a complete rejection of religion's role in society. Instead, many colonists started advocating for freedom as a fundamental pillar of fair governance. This concept is clearly illustrated in the Virginia Statute for Religious Freedom written by Thomas Jefferson, which served as the foundation for the First Amendment of the U.S. Constitution. The statute proclaimed that freedom of thought was a right that greatly influenced the young nation.

Despite these ideas of liberty and self-governance gaining momentum, they did not always apply to everyone. Enslaved Africans, Indigenous peoples, and other marginalized groups were often excluded from these enlightened principles. Their stories, struggles, and aspirations for freedom were under-currents that existed alongside the dominant narrative of this period. Their experiences serve as a reminder that the journey toward liberty was far from straightforward or universally inclusive; it was a path marked by contradictions, exclusions, and ongoing challenges.

As we come to a close in this chapter, we reflect upon this era of diversity with an understanding of its intricacies. The colonies formed a legacy of faiths, practices, and beliefs – each leaving an indelible impact on the culture and politics of that time.

From the waves of the Great Awakening to the unwavering resilience of faith amidst immense hardship, the colonial era served as a crucible where the foundation of a future nation was shaped. It was not only within chambers or through vocal demonstrations but also in sacred gatherings and heartfelt prayers that the very identity of this nation took form. The seeds planted during this period—freedom, individual conscience, and human rights—would continue to blossom into principles that fueled a revolution and challenged the newborn country to uphold its loftiest ideals.

Exploring the Role of African Americans and Other Minority Groups in the Colonial Era

African Americans and various minority groups

As we delve into the known narratives that weave through the vibrant fabric of colonial life, we uncover stories that have been relegated to mere footnotes in history books. These stories encompass African Americans, Native Americans, and other minority groups that play a role in understanding the broad spectrum of colonial existence.

A vast landscape of a Virginia plantation at dusk. Enslaved African Americans are seen tending to tobacco f

In this scene, it's clear that colonial Boston was far from an egalitarian society. Enslaved individuals and indentured servants, often living under harsh conditions, coexisted in a social hierarchy underpinning the complexities of race, freedom, and bondage in America.

Among the individuals we encounter is a man named Onesimus from Africa whose life story sheds light on complex circumstances. Despite being enslaved and brought to Boston, Onesimus played a role in a significant advancement in public health during that era: smallpox inoculation. Remarkably, even though he was enslaved, Onesimus shared his knowledge from Africa with his owner, Cotton Mather. This knowledge eventually saved lives. His story, like others, highlights the paradoxical nature of a society that both oppressed and relied upon those it had subjugated.

Now, shifting our focus from the ports to the regions, we come across the Native American experience during this period characterized by resilience and adaptation. Despite enduring challenges posed by European settlement, such as land displacement, diseases, and escalating conflicts, Native communities strove to preserve their cultural heritage and maintain their autonomy. They engaged in trade activities, formed alliances with groups, and occasionally mounted fierce resistance against colonial encroachment.

One particular tale of resistance revolves around Metacom King Philip among the Wampanoag people. Through his leadership during King Philip's War—a conflict between inhabitants and English colonists—Metacom exemplified the struggle of Native Americans to protect their way of life. The war inflicted loss of life and stability while serving as a stark reminder of underlying tensions simmering beneath the surface of colonial expansion.

Meanwhile, women from different backgrounds faced their own set of unique challenges during the colonial period. Even in a patriarchal society, women played vital roles by running businesses, managing households, and actively shaping colonial culture. However, their significant contributions were often undervalued due to limited rights and societal expectations that they had to navigate.

Resilience and influence

As dusk descends upon a plantation in Virginia, long shadows stretch across fields that have endured labor under the oppressive system of chattel slavery. Enslaved African Americans were responsible for cultivating cash crops such as tobacco, rice, and indigo that fueled the economy. Their influence extended beyond labor. They also brought vibrant cultural traditions, knowledge, and skills forever imprinting American culture.

Among these individuals, we come across Ayuba Suleiman Diallo, also known as Job Ben Solomon, an educated Muslim hailing from present-day Senegal. After being abducted and sold into slavery in Maryland, Diallo displayed resilience, eventually leading to his freedom and return home. His unique narrative offers firsthand accounts of African life and slavery from an African perspective. Diallo's autobiography is a treasure that grants us insight into the intellect and spirituality of an enslaved African, challenging prevalent stereotypes.

Alongside the struggles faced by African Americans, numerous other marginalized communities experienced discrimination in the colonies. The growing population consisted of enslaved Africans, Native Americans, and immigrants from countries like Ireland, Germany, and later on, Jewish communities from Eastern Europe and Portugal. This diverse blend contributed to a social fabric.

Multiculturalism thrived in cities such as New York and Philadelphia in the North. The streets echoed with various languages while tantalizing aromas wafted through the air from different cuisines. Traditional attire painted a picture at every turn. However, beneath this rich cultural tapestry lay inequalities that could not be ignored. Voting rights were typically limited to men who owned property, consequently leaving women economically disadvantaged and all minority groups disenfranchised. Despite these limitations, communities found spaces to maintain a sense of independence and strength. Synagogues like Shearith Israel in New York, founded in 1654, offered comfort and support for Jewish settlers, although most Sephardic Jews arrived in the late 17th century.

In addition, women, those who were single or widowed, occasionally took on roles that went beyond societal expectations. Some became "husbands" taking charge of their husband's businesses during their absence. Some engaged in small-scale commerce as "petty traders". Despite their legal rights, their economic activities played a critical role in the colonial economy and the well-being of their communities.

Interwoven throughout these stories of resilience are the relationships between enslaved Africans or African Americans and Native Americans. Some Native American tribes, affected by the need for labor due to diseases with devastating impacts on their populations, participated in the slave trade. On the other hand, there were instances where African Americans and Native Americans found common ground, leading to intermarriage and shared communities. This fusion contributed to the fabric that makes up American identity.

Contribution to America's social, cultural, and political landscape

The moon casts a light across the scenery, symbolizing the transition and enduring optimism within the human spirit. As we delve deeper into the era, we must recognize the enduring legacy left by minority groups and their indelible mark on American society.

The rich musical traditions of communities resonated with the heartbeat of a people torn from their homelands. These rhythms and melodies evolved, influencing genres like spirituals, blues, and jazz, and later intersecting with other traditions to birth rock 'n' roll – profoundly shaping American music. The fusion of African culinary practices with local ingredients gave rise to soul food – a source of comfort during challenging times and a cause for celebration during happier moments.

Let us not forget the defiance in preserving cultural heritage; for instance, the African storytelling tradition served as an act of resistance by safeguarding history and moral values through oral narratives. The Gullah community, the descendants of Africans enslaved in the regions of the Carolinas and Georgia, still maintain their unique language and customs. This serves as a living testament to their resilience and cultural heritage.

The impact of their presence extends beyond culture. African expertise in agriculture, including knowledge of the land, crops, and cultivation techniques, drove the American economy forward. Enslaved Africans' skills were instrumental in establishing rice cultivation in the Carolinas, indigo production in Georgia, and various agricultural practices across the colonies.

Unfortunately, these valuable contributions often get overshadowed by the reality of slavery and systematic discrimination. Acknowledging this dichotomy between influence and oppression is crucial to grasp America's past and shape its future.

There is more to this story. A new era was dawning as whispers of Revolution began spreading among colonists' hearts. Ideas of liberty echoed through taverns and found their way into pamphlets. They ignited debates in town squares. These concepts held meaning not only for intellectual elites but also for marginalized individuals.

How did enslaved African Americans perceive calls for liberty? What about Native Americans witnessing continuous encroachment on their lands? These are questions that further enrich our understanding of history. What about the women responsible for managing farms, running businesses, and caring for their families, yet they were left out of the discussions? It's ironic. They were fighting for freedom from tyranny while simultaneously denying it to others.

The Foundation of Economy and Labor Structures

The colonial economy, the different labor systems, and the emerging capitalist structures

As the first rays of sunlight gently awaken the colonies, let us take a moment to observe our surroundings. The delightful scent of baked bread fills the air while blacksmith hammers create a rhythmic melody and eager merchants open their stores. This vibrant economic scene did not simply materialize out of the air; it was a culmination of years of hard work, inventiveness, and a system that offered opportunities alongside exploitation.

Illustrated bustling colonial town at sunrise, showcasing activities such as blacksmithing, baking, and tradi

The economic heartbeat of the colonies was incredibly diverse, reflecting the geography and resources found in this New World. Picture, in your mind's eye, a map not defined by boundaries or borders. Instead, it showcases the pulsating economic lifeblood that characterized early America.

The Northern colonies thrived on activities like shipbuilding, fishing, lumbering, and small-scale farming. The colonies grew crops such as wheat, barley, and rye, which earned them the nickname "the breadbasket". In the South, things moved slowly but with great strength. The landscape is dominated by plantations that rely on enslaved Africans for labor. These plantations produce tobacco, rice, and indigo. Crops that require labor but offer significant rewards.

This economic diversity brought both advantages and disadvantages. On the one hand, it allowed each region to reduce dependence on external imports. It also fostered a sense of regional identity. However, it also created divisions due to differing interests. These divisions would become a source of conflict in the United States for many years.

Beneath this regional diversity lies a common factor: the rise of capitalism. The colonies were established initially as ventures with profit in mind. Shareholders from lands eagerly awaited investment returns, driving the colonial economy with an unwavering pursuit of profit. In this system, labor played a vital role as the driving force behind various activities such as crop harvesting, shipbuilding, and rum distillation— the demand for labor created structures that had unique implications for society.

One of these structures was indentured servitude. Imagine an Englishman, filled with hope but lacking funds, signing a contract to work for a colonial master for a fixed period, typically five to seven years. In return, they would receive passage to America, accommodation, food, and sometimes even land as "freedom dues" upon completing their service. It may have seemed like a mutually beneficial agreement. Was it?

The reality was often harsh for indentured servants. They endured rude conditions, and while some managed to gain their freedom and thrive afterward, others were not as fortunate. Sadly, many did not survive their period of servitude due to illness, lack of nutrition, or mistreatment. It is important to remember that this system operates on participation. Nonetheless, we must also consider those who had no choice.

Ideological tensions

As time passed during the century, the American colonies found themselves in the middle of a whirlwind of economic, social, and ideological changes. Despite being under the rule, each colony gradually developed its distinctive American identity through shared experiences shaped by struggles for survival, economic expansion, and navigating complex social hierarchies.

Though distinct, the colonies' economies were becoming increasingly interconnected. The Southern colonies specialized in tobacco, rice, and indigo production, while the Northern colonies focused on shipping and manufacturing goods as producing foodstuffs and raw materials. This interdependence of their economies acted as a bond among them all. Fostering a shared destiny would ultimately culminate in their united pursuit of independence. However, not everyone experienced prosperity equally. The rich became wealthier, the landowners and merchants, while many others, including small farmers, laborers, indentured servants, and enslaved individuals, struggled to make ends meet. These economic disparities created tensions that eventually led to the Revolutionary War.

The colonies also served as a breeding ground for ideas. The Enlightenment was not limited to Europe; it permeated life. Books and newspapers were more accessible due to advances in printing technology, allowing ideas to spread quickly. Coffeehouses and pubs buzzed with conversations about politics and philosophy. It was a time of awakening that prompted discussions questioning authority, liberty, and rights.

Think of these ideas as streams flowing through the intellectual world. Over time, they merged into a mighty river that would wash away the old order. Benjamin Franklin perfectly embodied this spirit of curiosity and defiance against traditional authority. As a printer, scientist, and statesman, he nurtured a culture of inquiry and debate that became integral to the American ethos. Furthermore, a religious revival known as the Great Awakening impacted the colonies during the 1730s and 1740s. This movement questioned the established order and advocated for a more personal and emotional connection with divinity. It resulted in the diminished influence of churches and clergy, fostering a democratic spirit in religious practices. Individuals were encouraged to read the Bible and seek truth for themselves.

These religious ideas, which emphasized agency and skepticism towards authority, intertwined with Enlightenment principles to shape a distinct American identity. This identity became rooted in values such as individualism, freedom, and questioning sources of authority. It wasn't just intellectual or spiritual forces that propelled the colonies towards the Revolution, but also the practical matters of economic policies. This included stricter trade regulations, the imposition of taxes, and limitations on colonial manufacturing—deeply frustrated colonists who lacked representation in the British Parliament.

By the mid-18th century, these various economic, social, and ideological changes had coalesced into discontent. The stage was set for challenging existing norms and Revolution. It's important to note that revolutions do not occur suddenly; they are born out of processes over time. They had been shaped by decades of mounting tension, and the colonies were approaching their breaking point.

4

Toward Independence and Revolutionary War (1754–1784)

The Ideological and International Contexts of Revolution 1754–1774

Root ideologies and global influences

Step into history, where the threads of experiences, ambitions, and the relentless march of time intertwine. We can sense the tangible tension and restless desire for change as we run our fingers along the patterns representing 1754 to 1774. The winds of Revolution surged through these two decades, shaping historical events and breathing life into countless individuals and communities daring to challenge the world as they knew it.

Our tale doesn't commence with a declaration or a single act of defiance; instead, it unfolds within an atmosphere imbued with the transformation that seeped through each of the thirteen colonies.

Imagine, if you can, the lively sound of horse hooves echoing on streets paved with cobblestones, the buzz of activity in bustling marketplaces, and the soft rustle of handwritten pamphlets passed from one person to another. These sounds marked the birth of an idea that would eventually rock the foundations of colonial America.

Illustration of the streets of colonial America from 1754 to 1774

When discussing the origins of the American Revolution, it is essential to mention the Enlightenment. This remarkable era of reason and intellectual rebellion originated in Europe, where its influence spread across the Atlantic Ocean. Think of Enlightenment ideas as seeds carried by winds and finding ground in the minds of American colonists. The works and philosophies of thinkers such as John Locke, Jean Jacques

Rousseau, and Baron de Montesquieu were not merely concepts confined to distant European salons lit by candlelight. On the contrary, their words traversed oceans resonated within town squares, and found their place on bookshelves in this New World. They inspired people who began perceiving their society, government, and entire existence through a new perspective of self-governance and individual rights.

To illustrate this point further, let's consider John Locke—a philosopher whose writings can be seen as fuel for what ignited the American spirit. He advocated that government functioned as a social agreement between those in power and those being governed. Moreover, he asserted that individuals possessed inherent rights to life, freedom, and property, which no monarch could violate with impunity.

Now, to understand the impact of these ideas, let your mind conjure an image of a colonist, perhaps a farmer or a shoemaker, absorbed in reading these words while bathed in the gentle glow of a crackling fireplace. Envision the emotions within his heart as he begins to question the unquestionable authority of kings. He gradually embraces the belief that he possesses inherent entitlements and is not merely a subject but an esteemed citizen. This paradigm shift was momentous, akin to plates realigning within the realm of human consciousness. Then came the Great Awakening, a robust religious revival that had recently swept through the colonies. In its wake emerged a populace imbued with individualism and skepticism towards secular and ecclesiastical authorities. Visualize impassioned sermons in revival gatherings amid fervent prayers in various languages, including English, African tongues, and Native

American dialects. This movement was more than religious; it signified individuals reclaiming personal autonomy while asserting that anyone, not solely ordained figures, could seek their divine truth.

During the mid-18th century, there was a period of power struggles among European nations. War and diplomacy became a perpetual cycle for these great powers. The Seven Years' War (1756–1763), known as the French and Indian War in America, was a monumental conflict spanned multiple continents. It touched everything from the forests of North America to the palaces of Europe, even reaching the fragrant spice markets of India.

In the colonies, this war unfolded as a brutal battle on the frontier. British and colonial soldiers fought against French forces and their Native American allies. Just picture it: regulars in their red coats, colonial militias proudly wearing blue and buff uniforms, and Native American warriors adorned with vibrant war paint. All clashing amidst the lush wilderness that defined the American frontier.

But this war went beyond territorial disputes; it played a crucial role in shaping colonial identity. Men from different colonies fought side by side, forming bonds through shared experiences. Picture a rifleman, a Massachusetts grenadier, and a Mohawk scout gathered around the same campfire on a crisp night. Their voices blend as they break bread and shed blood for their cause. In those moments, they were not Virginians, people from Massachusetts, or Mohawks; they embodied something new and undefined yet unquestionable.

Yet, wars come at a cost, and the Seven Years' War left Britain with an expanded empire but depleted coffers. The British government, situated across an intimidating ocean, turned to its prosperous offspring: the colonies. To replenish their financial resources, these policies sparked discontent among colonists, who viewed them as unjust and contradictory to their developing sense of rights and identity.

"No taxation without representation!"

During the years after 1754, significant changes swept across the colonies. These changes brought not only the ideas of the Enlightenment and echoes of spiritual revival but also the seeds of discord planted by an empire struggling to maintain control over its distant territories. This period can be likened to a moment before a symphony reaches its crescendo, filled with brewing storms and whispers of rebellion. The atmosphere was charged with potential and tension, creating a mixture that promised—or threatened—to bring about profound transformations.

The British grappled with the debt incurred during the Seven Years' War and the vastness of their empire, where daylight never ceased to shine. However, sustaining such an empire came at a significant cost. Picture yourself in London parlors, where wig-wearing British parliamentarians debated strengthening their strained treasury. The solution they ultimately settled upon would set them on a collision course with their subjects—taxation. Despite these growing sentiments, the British government's actions further fanned the flames of colonial dissent, particularly with the introduction of the

Stamp Act.

In 1764, the British government implemented the Sugar Act, which reduced tax rates on molasses but introduced measures to ensure effective tax collection to combat widespread smuggling within the colonies. This was followed by the Currency Act, which forbade the colonies from issuing their paper money. Now, picture the colonists who were already used to having a level of self-governance suddenly facing limitations in their familiar pathways of trade and currency. Guess the frustration and powerlessness that grew in their hearts. It was not only an attack on their finances but on their sense of identity.

The Stamp Act of 1765 ignited colonial resistance. This law mandated that various printed materials in the colonies be produced on stamped paper in London bearing a revenue stamp. Just concoct a world where items like newspapers, playing cards, diplomas, or legal documents are expensive—a tangible reminder of how a distant government exerted control over your daily life.

What's important to grasp is that these taxes alone were not excessively burdensome compared to contemporary British taxes. It was the underlying principle that stung. The idea was that a government across the ocean could dip its hands into the pockets of people without representation within its halls of power. This upset and rubbed against the independent spirit flourishing in America's colonies.

"No taxation without representation!" quickly became the rallying cry, perfectly summarizing the colonists' deep sense of injustice. Imagine the scenes of protests, where people from all walks of life, regardless of wealth or status, stood united against the rule. Visualize the symbolism of burning effigies, impassioned speeches, and a growing sense of solidarity that joined individuals from diverse backgrounds into a force greater than their parts.

In 1765, the Stamp Act Congress convened in response to the Stamp Act, marking an unprecedented historical moment. While the Congress itself did not directly repeal the act, it voiced a formal protest against it, which played a pivotal role in its eventual repeal. There was a collective and coordinated response to British policies for the first time—a glimmer of a budding national identity emerging amidst joint dissent. Envision these delegates passionately debating and crafting their firm rebuke to the Crown. They were no longer Virginians, New Yorkers, or Pennsylvanians; they were beginning to perceive themselves as Americans.

As time progressed from the 1760s into the 1770s, tensions escalated. The tragic turning point came with the Boston Massacre in 1770 when British soldiers fatally shot five civilians. Picture a scene in Boston where the streets are covered in snow and an atmosphere filled with anger and fear. You can hear the sound of gunfire and the thud of bodies hitting the ground. This incident, broadcast across the colonies and beyond, solidified the growing conflict by portraying the British as oppressors and the colonists as defenders of liberty.

In rooms and bustling taverns, through letters written by candlelight and pamphlets passed eagerly from one person to another, ideas continued to spread. The writings of figures like Thomas Paine and Samuel Adams fueled a desire for something radical that had never been attempted— independence.

Illustration of the Boston Massacre in 1770

As we pause here, picture yourself standing atop a hill as night falls, overlooking all thirteen colonies. Observe the flickering glow of fires below and witness people gathering together in shadows and exchanging thoughts and information. Experience the restlessness in the air – a collective energy building up, a shared purpose taking shape. The stage was set; all players were readying themselves; it was time for the Revolution to unfold.

American colonies desire for independence

In the atmosphere of the 1770s, the American colonies were like a powder keg, eagerly awaiting a catalyst for the Revolution. The ideals brewing for some time now turned into action, and resistance led to unity. However, amid this uprising, it is essential to note that not all colonists were revolutionaries. Loyalties were divided; opinions varied greatly. This movement was not a monolith but a chorus of different voices trying to find their place in an uncertain world.

The year 1773 witnessed an act of defiance so dramatic and symbolic that it left an indelible mark on history: the Boston Tea Party. This scene on a December night with the scent of salt and freedom permeating the air around 60 men. Some, disguised as Mohawk Native Americans, boarded ships in Boston Harbor. They didn't carry weapons. Instead, they had an unwavering passion for justice. And their method of protest wasn't violence; it was tea. They threw crate after crate of tea into the waters of the harbor.

Why did they choose tea, you might ask? This event was a response to the Tea Act, which was viewed as another way for the British to maintain control. It wasn't solely about tea. It was about standing up for principles. It was about a people asserting that they wouldn't submit to tyranny and silently watch their rights being eroded. They chose tea because it represented something like a daily source of comfort—and there's a particular strength in reclaiming the ordinary and declaring that even something as simple as a cup of tea is subject to the people's will.

The Boston Tea Party didn't go unanswered. In retaliation, the British introduced what became known as the Coercive Acts—a series of measures that included closing Boston Harbor and revoking certain rights from the Massachusetts colony. These acts aimed to isolate Boston and serve as an example but ironically achieved the opposite effect. Instead of extinguishing the fire, they only fueled it, and support poured in from colonies nearby. This was the environment in which the First Continental Congress came together in 1774 with representatives from twelve of the thirteen colonies, with Georgia not sending delegates. Visualize it: debates filling the air, heavy decisions weighing on everyone's minds, and walls echoing with passionate arguments and whispered conversations. These were men with diverse opinions, but they shared a common objective. They convened, discussed, and ultimately achieved a unified agreement to boycott British goods and a petition to the King—a united front against adversity.

The wheels of the Revolution had already been set in motion and could not be quickly halted. On the night of April 18, 1775, several riders, including Paul Revere, William Dawes, and Dr. Samuel Prescott, raced through the darkness to warn the colonies of the approaching British troops. Popular history often remembers Paul Revere's midnight ride—a moment deeply ingrained in American folklore—with phrases like "The British are coming!" Nonetheless, given the presence of British patrols and the need for discretion, the riders likely conveyed the warning in more subdued terms, possibly using phrases like "The Regulars are out!" Regardless of the exact words, this critical mission alerted the colonies to the imminent threat. The battles of Lexington and Concord swiftly followed on April 19, as muskets cracked and wills clashed at dawn, marking the beginning of armed conflict.

These initial volleys marked the beginning of a prolonged war, heralding a period of strife and struggle as the colonies sought to establish themselves as a nation. Before we move forward, let us take a moment to contemplate the significance of these events. A revolution is no small matter; it is characterized by upheaval, chaos, and a complete disruption of what was once familiar. It is an amalgamation of grievances and an overwhelming demand for change. It encompasses the clash of arms on battlefields and the silent determination of individuals who firmly believe there must be a path forward. The American Revolution contained all these aspects—it was a tableau painted with ideals and bloodshed, unity, and division; it involved ordinary people stepping onto the stage of history.

These initial shots, later described by Ralph Waldo Emerson as 'the shots heard round the world,' marked a turning point; we are poised to delve deeper into the Revolution itself: its battles, diplomacy efforts, heroic figures, and countless unnamed individuals who all played their part in birthing a new nation.

The Fight for Independence, Embracing Diversity in Battle 1775–1784

Inclusive nature of the struggle and the international stage

The War of Independence was much more than a clash between colonial minutemen and British soldiers in red coats. It was a transformation that reshaped political ideologies, individual rights, and even our understanding of what a nation could be. As we delve into this chapter, you can hear the sound of drums as families huddled together by candlelight, diplomats busily writing urgent letters with quills, and the world watching with anticipation...

1775, the air was heavy, with gunpowder and high expectations. The Battles of Lexington and Concord marked the beginning of the war, while the Second Continental Congress gathered in May. Let's take a moment to reflect on who these rebels indeed were. They were more than the famous individuals whose faces are on our money and whose names are seen throughout our cities. Among them were also those who often went unnoticed: women, Native Americans, African Americans, and people from all walks of life. They all came together at this moment in history, some by choice and others by circumstance.

Take, for example, Crispus Attucks—a man of African and Native American heritage—who became the first casualty of the Boston Massacre and thus a symbol of the growing Revolution. Another remarkable figure is Peter Salem, an enslaved person who fought bravely at Concord and the Battle of Bunker Hill. We mustn't overlook the countless women like Deborah Sampson, who disguised herself as a man to serve in the Continental Army, or Molly Pitcher, who took her husband's position at a cannon after he fell in battle.

Illustration of a bustling scene showing the multi-faceted nature of the Revolutionary War era

The Continental Army itself, under the leadership of General George Washington, was a group representing all thirteen colonies. While initially consisting mainly of New Englanders, it eventually included soldiers from every colony. This army was far from an organized machine; it often appeared disheveled, with limited supplies, training deficiencies, and occasional food shortages. Something immeasurable fueled their determination—an intangible sense of purpose and destiny.

Participation in the war went beyond the battlefield. African Americans, whether free or enslaved, found ways to get involved. Some joined the fight because they were promised freedom, while others served as spies, messengers, or in support roles. Similarly, many women expected to stick to roles also found ways to contribute by becoming nurses, spies, or maintaining the home front. Their everyday resilience was just as crucial to the war effort as any battle.

While battles raged on, another kind of war was happening – a war of words and alliances. This conflict extended beyond the thirteen colonies and reached across oceans. The young nation sent diplomats like Benjamin Franklin and John Adams to Europe to seek support from powers, primarily France. These diplomatic efforts required maneuvering because the world was like a chessboard of empires, and the American Revolution represented a major gamble on a global scale.

The international nature of the war is best exemplified by Marquis de Lafayette, an aristocrat inspired by the American cause. He willingly volunteered for service in the Continental Army. His influence played a vital role in securing additional support from France. Young and idealistic, he represented how interconnected the American Revolution was with a larger world that saw shifting alliances and shared Enlightenment ideals.

In the days of 1776, the talk of independence grew louder and more robust. A committee of five individuals, including Thomas Jefferson, John Adams, and Benjamin Franklin, was appointed by the Continental Congress to craft a declaration. The outcome was not a litany of grievances against the British Crown; it served as a manifesto for a fresh perspective on governance. It began with the words, "We hold these truths to be self-evident, that all men are created equal…"

This document, written during the scorching summer heat of 1776, was revolutionary in its content and ideas. It put forward a concept that a government's legitimacy stems from the consent of its citizens—a seismic shift in a world accustomed to kings claiming divine authority. While it did not provide a blueprint for this new form of government, it served as an assurance for a future that those rebelling were ready to fight for.

When the Declaration was officially adopted on July 4, 1776, it marked the expression of Revolution—a clear line drawn in the sand. There was no turning from that point onward. The ensuing struggle went beyond military conflict; it became a crucible that tested the principles outlined in that cherished document.

Now, let us take a moment to ponder upon how inclusive this conflict was. The Revolutionary War was far more than a conflict fought on battlefields. It was a struggle involving people from all walks of life across regions and cultures. It had a global impact, touching the lives of individuals and communities alike. As we delve into its history, we will witness how this inclusivity and diversity played a pivotal role in shaping the tumultuous progress of the Revolution.

Revolutionary War

The Revolutionary War was an intricate medley of human endeavors and sacrifices. It extended beyond battles; it encompassed strategies employed with desperation and moments of courage that became inseparable threads in our narrative fabric. These battles were crucibles where this nation's mettle was tested – where its future was written with bloodshed and gunpowder.

While hostilities like the Battles of Lexington and Concord had already begun, the Declaration of Independence formalized the colonies' intentions and intensified the reality of war. The British forces posed a challenge with their experienced troops and abundant resources. New York witnessed an early clash during the war known as the Battle of Long Island in August 1776. It was one of the most significant battles of the entire war, and the scene was filled with chaos. Picture thousands of soldiers locked in combat, smoke filling the air, and ground shaking from cannon blasts. The Continental Army, facing maneuvering and firepower, suffered a devastating defeat. This marked a moment to test George Washington's leadership skills as he orchestrated a nighttime retreat to save most of his army for future battles.

This story wasn't about glory or heroic triumphs. Instead, it was a tale of resilience, learning from setbacks, and enduring through the moments. By the end of 1776, the Revolution was hanging by a thread. The Continental Army was besieged; their numbers dwindled while morale sank as winter approached.

Then came a glimmer of hope—a daring gamble! On Christmas night in 1776, Washington led his troops across the ice-choked Delaware River. The morning brought an unexpected assault on Hessian forces in Trenton, New Jersey. Although not strategically significant on a scale, this victory had monumental implications for revitalizing the spirit of the Revolution.

The enduring image of Washington standing firm in a boat amidst fierce snow and ice captures the essence of unwavering determination against overwhelming odds.

Battles and generals did not solely define the war; it also encompassed the players and uncelebrated acts of bravery. Spies played a role, with An agent known by the code number 355 from the Culper Spy Ring was particularly renowned. However, their true identity remains a mystery. Additionally, James Armistead Lafayette, an enslaved American in Virginia, served as a double agent and provided vital information contributing to the eventual triumph at Yorktown. At the same time, the international chess match persisted. 1778 marked a turning point when France officially entered the conflict as an ally to America, mainly due to Benjamin Franklin's tireless diplomacy in Paris. Frances' involvement was partly driven by their desire for vengeance against Britain following their defeat in the Seven Years' War. This alliance brought supplies, financial aid, naval support, and military expertise. Spain also joined forces against Britain, transforming a rebellion into a global conflict.

Over the years, the war continued to rage on. Key battles unfolded in Saratoga and the harsh winter at Valley Forge, where the Continental Army faced conditions but became a more united and disciplined force. This was partly due to the training provided by Baron von Steuben, a military officer.

Let us not forget that this war affected more than those who held muskets or waved flags. Throughout the colonies, men, women, and children endured hardships. Women took charge of running households and businesses managing farms, and some even followed the army camps as "camp followers" to provide support services. Enslaved individuals sought freedom by escaping to lines or joining the fight for survival and hope amidst all the chaos.

As we bring this part to a close, envision the faces of those involved in the Revolution: farmers taking up arms, enslaved mothers courageously running towards freedom with their children, French noblemen fighting for a foreign land, and young women disguising themselves as male soldiers. Each individual had their reasons for being part of this conflict. Their unique definition of what freedom truly meant. Their intertwined narratives weave together to create a complex mix of a revolution that surpassed mere warfare; it was a gripping human drama with immense stakes unfolding against the backdrop of America's lush fields, quaint towns, and rugged wilderness landscapes.

Peace, global influences

The Revolutionary War, a mix of hope, despair, and unwavering determination, steadily marched towards its climactic moment. By 1781, the strain of battle had worn down both sides. Despite occupying cities, the British could not extinguish the indomitable American spirit that thrived in the countryside they couldn't control. Meanwhile, the Continental Army had been hardened through battles and was prepared for an ultimate confrontation.

So it begins at Yorktown in Virginia. Lord Charles Cornwallis, leading the forces, chose this location for its defensible position and anticipated reinforcements from the sea. Yet, fate would not favor them this time, as their expected naval support failed to materialize. Under Admiral de Grasse's leadership, the French fleet ensured the British naval support was thwarted, establishing a vital blockade. At the time, Washington utilized clever misinformation and his newly gained French allies to guide his troops toward Yorktown.

Let me tell you that the Siege of Yorktown was not just a battle but a remarkable display of cooperation and strategy. The unlikely allies. The French and American forces. Now, they stood together, digging trenches and establishing artillery positions. Enough, a relentless onslaught of fire and iron rained upon the British positions.

On October 19, 1781, Cornwallis was besieged without hope for relief. A the mixture of disbelief and euphoria among the ranks, the proud satisfaction in the French camp, and the resigned frustration within British tents. A nation born out of struggle and defined by its spirit had successfully turned the tide against one of history's most formidable empires.

Moreover, it's important to note that while the Siege of Yorktown marked the last significant military engagement, hostilities and minor skirmishes continued for some time. Skirmishes continued while diplomacy took the stage. Delicate negotiations involving diplomats from America, Britain, France, and Spain were required for The Treaty of Paris (1783). The world held its breath until reaching an agreement recognizing the United States' independence and laying the foundations for its westward expansion.

The Treaty of Paris was an agreement to end the war between Britain and its American colonies

The American Revolutionary War was not simply confined to America; it had an impact shaped by international alliances, strategic interests, and the complex geopolitical landscape of that era. The French played a role by providing military aid, financial support through loans, and naval power. The Spanish and Dutch also opened new fronts and offered vital economic resources. In fact, at its core, this war belonged to the people. Men and women from all walks of life participated in this effort, including free or enslaved Native American immigrants – each driven by their unique motivations. Some sought freedom, while others pursued opportunities. Many fought for their right to shape their destinies. The collective experiences of these individuals became the foundation upon which the United States was built.

At the end of this section, let us imagine a moment following the storm. Picture a soldier standing atop a hill after all is said and done – an ordinary individual whose name may not be recorded in history annals but whose contributions are invaluable. From this vantage point, he gazes across the land for which he fought tirelessly. His future is uncertain; however, he sees possibilities on the horizon – a vision that holds immense hope for what America could become. In this moment lies a spark that will ignite dreams for future generations.

The War of Independence went beyond a military clash; it represented a coming together of various aspirations and unwavering rebellions against the established global system. It served as a testament to the relentless human desire for self-governance, freedom, and the pursuit of happiness. This resilient spirit, forged through adversity and triumph, struggle and success, continues to form the identity's foundation.

III

BUILDING A NATION

5

From Confederation to Constitution (1784–1788)

The Shift and the Flaws of the Articles of Confederation

From the Articles of Confederation to the U.S. Constitution

After the dust settled following a war, the United States of America found itself standing amidst ancient nations. Picture post-war America: a collection of states with perspectives and governance brought together by a momentous revolution but untested in times of peace as a confederation. Historians often refer to this period as the 'Critical Period' when America faced existential threats not from external forces but from within its borders.

Imagine a nation governed by the Articles of Confederation, America's first attempt at a national constitution. Visualize it not as a structure but as loosely connected threads struggling to maintain unity among states under an umbrella of 'firm friendship.'

Ratified during the war in 1781, the Articles presented a structure contradictory to the idea of a strong central government. This was mainly because the memories of tyranny still lingered in people's minds.

18th-century public square in America. Groups gather around arguing for the ratification of the Constitution

Under these Articles, each state maintained sovereignty, freedom, and independence. It may sound perfect on the surface, right? Consider this: a governing body called the Continental Congress lacked the power to enforce laws, regulate trade, or impose taxes. A government desperately seeking funds to settle war debts while having a military force that was more symbolic than effectively protective. Additionally, states set up trade barriers against each other as if they were countries.

It wasn't a mere government; it was an intricate puzzle. How does a nation newly freed from control create a government that ensures liberty but is also capable enough to govern? How can it safeguard the fought rights while uniting diverse peoples and beliefs under one common flag?

In the years following the Revolution, they witnessed chaos. Think of those soldiers returning from battlefields as heroes for their nation but receiving payment in promissory notes instead of real money if you can picture it. Visualize steadfast farmers who embodied American identity, drowning in debt and facing imprisonment or losing their deserved lands.

Can you hear the murmurs of dissatisfaction and disappointment with a revolution that held high promises but seemed to deliver so little? One instance of this disillusionment peaked in the Shays Rebellion (1786- 1787). Daniel Shays, a war veteran and farmer, became the symbol of this revolt. However, it's important to remember that he wasn't an anomaly; he represented a sentiment. He and his group of Massachusetts farmers burdened by debts and unfair legal actions stood defiantly against what they saw as an unjust system. They weren't extremists; they were people – fathers, sons, and brothers – pushed to their limits demanding justice.

Shays Rebellion was not a localized protest; it resonated nationally and sparked urgent conversations in meeting halls, taverns, and homes across the states. The change was necessary. There was growing support for a convention to revise the

Articles of Confederation in this crisis atmosphere. Initially, the intent was to amend the failing Articles of Confederation, but deliberations eventually led to the drafting an entirely new document. Yet, history often takes turns. Leaders emerged during this period – individuals we now revere as our Founding Fathers.

Philadelphia Convention

In the summer of 1787, Philadelphia became the backdrop for deep reflection and discussion. It was when brilliant minds came together in debates, driven by their diverse perspectives. Picture James Madison, the Virginian advocating for a strong central government. Visualize Alexander Hamilton, the Federalist, engaging in clashes with figures like Patrick Henry, an ardent supporter of states' rights.

A depicted scene set in the late 18th century. Individuals poring over documents, including The Federalist Paper

As anticipation and anxiety filled the air leading up to the Philadelphia convention, their republic's fate hung precariously in the balance. Would this assembly of giants and conflicting egos be able to chart a path forward? Would their beloved nation splinter into oblivion?

Join us as we step into the revered halls of the Philadelphia Convention. These remarkable individuals debated fervently and shaped what would become known as the United States Constitution.

Visualize a city filled with excitement and anticipation where 55 delegates from various backgrounds gather at the Pennsylvania State House. Originally intended to revise the Articles of Confederation, this meeting would ultimately reshape the nation's future. These delegates were not just architects of a document, but instead, they held the destiny of a whole country in their hands.

Step inside the hall and witness this assembly yourself; feel the moment's weight. Each delegate represented their state's interests, fully aware that compromise was not merely an option but an absolute necessity for survival. Among these individuals were luminaries whose impact still reverberates today. There was George Washington, revered as a hero of the Revolution, his presence lending both gravity and unity to these proceedings. James Madison was also present— the "Father of the Constitution"—whose ideas and skilled politicking left an indelible mark on history. Let's not forget Alexander Hamilton, whose bold vision of a strong centralized government greatly influenced these debates.

Notably, this Convention was far from harmonious; instead, it resembled a symphony reflecting America's diverse tapestry. Picture those debates; one side proposing the Virginia Plan advocating for a powerful central government with representation based on population—a proposition that pitted larger states against smaller ones. On the side stood the New Jersey Plan, countering with equal representation for each state.

The Great Compromise, also known as the Connecticut Compromise, skillfully crafted by Roger Sherman, brought together these plans to create a two-house legislature that achieved a balance in representation. However, the disagreements ran deep. It affected the very essence of what the new nation would stand for. The haunting issue of slavery casting a shadow over the Convention sparked one of its most intense debates and controversial outcomes. Just picture the delegates, whose economies relied on this vile trade, clashing with their northern counterparts who advocated for its abolition. The resulting Three-Fifths Compromise, which counted enslaved people as three-fifths of a person for taxation and representation purposes, was not a proper resolution—it was a temporary solution to ease the pain of a growing wound that would eventually tear the nation apart many decades later.

Imagine being in that room—the charged atmosphere filled with arguments echoing off the walls—discussing presidential powers, balancing state and federal authority methods for electing officials, and concerns about anarchy and tyranny. In this battleground of ideas, they painstakingly crafted the United States Constitution—a resilient and adaptable document yet imperfect.

The Constitution emerged from that room, thick with tension and tobacco smoke, taking shape step by step as each article and clause were carefully constructed. It wasn't a document being created but rather a social agreement for the people of the United States. This agreement promised a system with a careful balance of powers and assurance of a Bill of Rights that would be added later. It also emphasized the principles of democracy and republicanism.

This was not the end of their challenges. The Constitution, born out of compromise, still faced scrutiny and judgment. As the Convention ended, the delegates were well aware that their work had just begun. The battle for ratification loomed ahead, and it would require their intelligence, determination, and deep knowledge to convince a population to embrace this new vision for America.

As the delegates departed the room in Philadelphia, the Constitution began its journey toward ratification. This journey will be filled with contention, ideological warfare, and an unwavering pursuit of a perfect union.

Ideological battles and public debates

The tale did not conclude with the ink drying on paper in Philadelphia; it was merely the beginning of a chapter. Envision the United States after the Convention, a nation standing at the edge of transformative change as the Constitution was sent to the states for approval. This moment was not about a legal document; it carried profound significance for the identity and essence of a young nation.

The ratification process is like a sea where waves of public opinion clash against established norms. Two distinct groups emerged from this storm: the Federalists, who embraced the Constitution, and their counterparts, known as Anti-Federalists, who opposed it. This disagreement went beyond differences; it represented an existential battle that shaped America's identity and potential.

Picture influential figures like Alexander Hamilton, James Madison, and John Jay leading the Federalist movement. They perceived a stronghold against chaos in the Constitution—a robust central government that would provide stability, unity, and progress. With enthusiasm, they took up their quills and penned a series of essays called The Federalist Papers—the talk of that era.

Picture this scene: ordinary Americans gathered by candle-light, eagerly absorbing arguments that are still relevant today. These discussions highlighted the importance of a central authority, the brilliance of the checks and balances system, and the potential for prosperity under unified governance.

Now, let's contrast this with a group known as the Anti-Federalists. This coalition included everyone from back-country farmers to educated elites who all shared one fear: suspicion. Influential leaders like Patrick Henry, Samuel Adams, and George Mason were concerned about the proposed Constitution. They worried that it could trample on liberties and pave the way for authoritarian rule—echoing memories of the oppression they had fought against during the Revolution. Their speeches, articles, and pamphlets flooded discourse with passionate warnings about a central government that might become too powerful, an absence of specific individual rights listed, and the potential erosion of state authority.

Amidst this clash of ideologies emerged something remarkable— a development not enforced by law or decree but driven by urgent voices within society. Here, the Bill of Rights came into being—the ten amendments to the Constitution—forged through intense public debate. These amendments served as a promise—a binding agreement with all Americans—that their freedoms would be protected and enshrined in writing.

Conceive the intensity—the anticipation mingled with anxiety—as each state convened conventions to deliberate on ratification. Imagine the scene in Massachusetts, a center of sentiment where the decision hung in the balance until leaders made promises to consider amendments that would protect individual rights, ultimately swaying the outcome. Similarly, in Virginia, James Madison's eloquence clashed with Patrick Henry's speeches, resulting in a battle of ideals.

Finally, on June 21, 1788, New Hampshire became the state to ratify the Constitution, marking its official implementation. Nevertheless, the drama didn't end there; it continued until Virginia and New York agreed to solidify the Union. As the last candles burned out and the final votes were counted, the United States emerged more robust and unified from this rigorous process. The nation didn't simply adopt a constitution; it underwent a thorough examination through public debates and discussions that forged a collective identity.

This was the beginning rather than the end. A new chapter awaited, filled with challenges, triumphs, and tragedies. With its ratified Constitution in place, America was ready to embark on its ambitious experiment—a test of its ideals and people's perseverance.

Crafting U.S. Constitution; Impacts on Women, Minorities, and Religious Groups

Societal consequences

With the ratification of the Constitution, a new era began in the United States. But who were the beneficiaries of this era? Whose lives were transformed – for better or worse – by the drafted principles governing this young nation? The story of the Constitution remains incomplete without acknowledging those often marginalized in records: women, minorities, and religious groups.

Picture a budding nation with soil nurtured by promises but tainted by contradictions. While the Constitution laid out a framework for equality and freedom, its implementation was inconsistent. The document embodied paradoxes as it was created by men who advocated for liberty while simultaneously supporting or tolerating slavery.

Women played roles during the Revolution, not only managing households but occasionally disguising themselves and joining the fight. However, when it came to the version of the Constitution, there was a notable absence of mention regarding women's rights. And Abigail Adams, wife of John

Adams, earnestly wrote letters to her husband urging him to consider women's interests in our nation's laws. While her words held significance, they seemed like a whisper amidst the overwhelming dominance of male politics. Regardless of their contributions, women were mostly confined to norms that dictated their roles, and their legal identities were overshadowed by their fathers or husbands.

Nevertheless, the winds of change began to stir yet persistently. Within households and communities, women shaped our nation through influence, education, and entrepreneurship rather than voting power. They served as roots that kept the Tree of Liberty firm amidst storms threatening its stability.

Now, let us shift our attention toward the blend of minority communities. For African Americans, the Constitution proved to be a double-edged sword. The infamous Three-Fifths Compromise acknowledged them as three-fifths of a person regarding representation—a painful reminder of their dehumanization—while simultaneously granting slave states greater power.

The Constitution did not allow the prohibition of the slave trade until after 1808, which created significant divisions for many years to follow. Not to mention, African Americans who were free in the States started to ignite resistance and foster a sense of community. Imagine churches as the heart of these communities, where free Black individuals formed their identity and collective strength. Their stories may have been concealed, but They played a crucial role in shaping our nation.

We must also consider the people who were the original inhabitants of this land. Although recognized as nations by the Constitution, they faced challenges due to expansionism. While their rights were acknowledged on paper, they often experienced marginalization in practice. Treaties between them and the U.S. Government were frequently undermined when they served convenience.

Lastly, let's focus on groups. The Constitution was groundbreaking in its dedication to freedom through its First Amendment, which prevented Congress from establishing any religion or restricting its exercise. This was a stance considering that religious persecution persisted worldwide—people of faith. Christians, Jews, and Quakers found America a sanctuary where diverse beliefs flourished, just like our vast land.

Personal experiences and societal changes

Notwithstanding the ideals enshrined in the Constitution, the everyday lives of individuals belonging to various communities reveal stories of resilience amidst systemic constraints. Let us step into their homes, traverse their streets, and listen to their whispers and pleas to comprehend this crucial period.

Regarding women's lives, notable figures like Mercy Otis Warren rose to prominence. Warren, a writer and propagandist during the Revolutionary War era, was not merely an observer but an active participant in shaping political ideologies. Not to mention, like women of her time, her influence remained an exception rather than the norm. Most women were engaged in what historians call "republican motherhood". The developing nation entrusted them with raising citizens—an indirect recognition of their significance in shaping the future—yet still within the confines of domestic life.

For African Americans, their reality was starkly distinct. Phyllis Wheatley, a talented poet who was unfortunately enslaved, wrote influential works that gained recognition on both sides of the Atlantic. Despite her fame and admiration for her intelligence, her daily life highlighted the contradictions of a nation proclaiming freedom for all. Additionally, nameless and faceless individuals toiled in the cotton fields, their sweat and blood marking every fiber of American history even though their stories have been lost.

At the same time, African Americans who were free yet lived in a world of their enslaved counterparts faced their struggles. They built schools, churches, and businesses to establish communities in a society that often treated them as second-class citizens. Their adventure is one of determination as they carve out a place for themselves against all odds.

For Native Americans during this era, it was a testament to their resilience in unrelenting adversity. Leaders such as Little Turtle from the Miami tribe and Joseph Brant from the Mohawk tribe balanced resistance and diplomacy as they fought to ensure a future for their people in an ever-changing world. It was a world where treaties lost their significance immediately after being signed; each day brought new uncertainties.

Religious minorities also found themselves intertwined with the framework of this young nation. Although the Constitution guaranteed freedom, the reality was more nuanced. For example, Catholics faced prejudice and suspicion due to lingering animosities from the Protestant majority. Nonetheless, influential figures like John Carroll, who became the Catholic bishop in the United States, played a crucial role in advocating for religious tolerance and laying the foundation for the future of Catholicism in our nation.

Despite their small numbers, Jewish Americans carved out a niche for themselves. Individuals like Haym Solomon played a part in financing the Revolutionary War and demonstrated unwavering patriotism. Yet, Jewish communities still faced societal prejudices, with their acceptance often conditional and their rights primarily protected locally rather than on a federal scale.

As these intertwined stories unfold, they create a mosaic that reflects American society after 1787. While the Constitution was a guiding principle, it was not a cure-all solution. Its ideals illuminated our path forward. Its omissions reverberated loudly through the lives it neglected.

Effects and setting the stage for challenges

In the parlors of Philadelphia, distinguished gentlemen gathered to create a Constitution to guide the young nation, leading it toward an unparalleled future in human history. On the other hand, hidden within this document's intricacies and unspoken words lay the lives of millions entangled in the whirlwind of an era in America.

For women during this time, it was a period of contradiction. While republican motherhood elevated their status as guardians of virtue, it did so within strict societal boundaries. John Adams's wife, Abigail Adams, captured this sentiment perfectly when she made her timeless plea; "Remember the ladies". Although her words carried a playful tone, they served as a stark reminder of the hopes and frustrations experienced by women. They influenced society to some extent. True political empowerment seemed like an unreachable peak amidst an imposing social landscape.

The Constitution remained silent on the issue of slavery. A silence that reverberated throughout the following decades. Enslaved individuals, deprived of autonomy, sought solace and resistance through various means. From subtle acts of defiance to heartfelt spiritual songs that whispered tales of freedom.

In the North, Black individuals like Paul Cuffee, who was successful in business and as a sea captain, demonstrated that determination and skill could overcome barriers. However, despite their successes, they still faced limitations.

For Native Americans, the Constitution seemed foreign. They provided little protection against the expanding wave of settlement. They were often not considered part of the community for which the Constitution was originally designed. Their diplomatic efforts, such as the Treaty of Fort Harmar in 1789, often resulted in the loss of land. This pattern. They left behind a trail of tears alongside their resilience.

Religious groups found some protection under the First Amendment, although it did not guarantee absolute freedom from prejudice. Within this legal framework, various faiths could take root in American soil. The story of Touro Synagogue, the oldest in the country, exemplifies this commitment to religious freedom with its heartfelt letter from George Washington ensuring liberty. It represents hope for a future despite facing challenges along the way.

As we approached the end of the century, while the Constitution had laid out its principles and structure for governance purposes, diverse individuals played different roles with their unique scripts that reflected the diversity of our nation.

The concepts of freedom and fairness were noble. They came with challenges and contradictions that everyday people – including women, enslaved individuals, free Black people, Native Americans, and religious minorities – had to navigate. This navigation involved moments of happiness and sorrow, hopes ignited and extinguished, all driven by a determination that would shape the United States. The parchment and quill were the beginning of our nation's rich history; as time unfolded, it became clear that the hunger for true equality and justice was insatiable, making the journey toward achieving them difficult. Throughout its early years, America was filled with promises yet marked by omissions. As we reflect on our past, we recognize our founding fathers' contributions and acknowledge the vital roles of founding mothers and communities – each thread weaving an unfinished tapestry together, each voice harmonizing in a symphony that is America.

Economic Factors in the Formation of the Constitution

Influences and debates that shaped the creation of the U.S. Constitution.

After the Revolutionary War, America had big aspirations but limited resources. When delegates gathered in Philadelphia during the summer of 1787, they faced various economic challenges that reflected the diversity and divisions among the states they represented. A palpable tension filled the air amid discussions about currency, taxes, trade, and war debts. The room where they debated, shielded from scrutiny, became a melting pot where different economic philosophies clashed and eventually came together to shape the country's Constitution.

The Debt Dilemma and Early Compromises

To begin with, one pressing issue was America's debt burden. The costs of fighting in the Revolutionary War had severely depleted reserves, leaving behind an enormous war debt that hung over everyone like a gloomy cloud. How to effectively manage this debt became a topic that sharply divided opinions.

The northern states, such as Massachusetts, had their share of debt and favored the federal government taking on state debts. On the other hand, southern states like Virginia, with lighter debt burdens, were reluctant to support the idea of federal assumption, seeing it as a reward for the excessive spending in the North.

An imagined port in the late 1780s. Deals negotiation, workers unload cargo, and officials oversee tariff collecti

Building on Hamilton's proposal for the federal assumption of state debts, tensions arose between states. The South, having lesser debt, expressed hesitations. They questioned why they should shoulder the burden of expenditures incurred by the North. In light of these concerns, an informal but crucial agreement known as the Dinner Table Bargain was reached; in exchange for support in assuming the debt, the nation's new capital would be moved southward and eventually settled along the Potomac River. This decision embodied the nation's dedication to balancing interests, a recurring theme throughout American history.

Debt was one piece of the economic puzzle. The Articles of Confederation had left the federal government powerless — to impose taxes and heavily dependent on voluntary contributions from individual states. The echoes of the Shays

Rebellion—an uprising in Massachusetts driven by economic hardships and burdensome taxes—still lingered in people's minds as a stark reminder of what could happen when a central authority lacks strength.

Bankruptcy was certainly not what our founding fathers had envisioned as their legacy. James Madison, an individual with a calm demeanor but an impressive intellect, put forward the Virginia Plan. This plan advocated a stronger central government empowered to make laws, impose taxes, and regulate trade. In contrast to the influential New Jersey Plan, this proposal set the stage for intense debates during the Convention.

The issue of commerce, vital for any nation's well-being, also became a topic. With states imposing tariffs on each other's goods and navigation acts restricting trade, tensions were high. The rural southern states heavily relied on slave labor and cash crop exports, while the industrializing northern states had merchants, manufacturers, and small farmers seeking protection and uniform trade regulations.

Amidst this cacophony of discussions emerged a crucial question: What kind of economy did this new nation envision as it embarked on its bold experiment in democracy?

As the Constitution was still being shaped, it needed to address these economic divisions. It had to balance state sovereignty and federal authority, local interests and national vision, and immediate needs versus aspirations. The debates among the delegates were passionate. They were heated as they recognized that their decisions would reverberate far beyond the confines of the convention hall.

The atmosphere in the room was charged with debates and the weight of uncertain futures. In one corner, Charles Pinckney from South Carolina passionately advocated for protecting states' rights regarding their economic policies. Nevertheless, proponents of power like Madison and Hamilton argued that without federal control over commerce and finances, there would be constant conflicts between states' economic policies, resulting in domestic and international instability and weakness.

Finding a compromise was an option and a necessity that emerged from heated debates. One such compromise was the Connecticut Compromise, also called the Great Compromise, which proposed a two-chamber legislature with representation in the House and equal representation in the Senate. However, it was the Commerce Compromise that ultimately resolved many economic disputes.

The federal government was granted the authority to regulate trade between states and countries, including imposing import tariffs. But, it was strictly prohibited from imposing taxes on exports.

This decision brought a sense of relief to the South, whose agricultural economy heavily relied on exporting goods. The North, aiming to safeguard its emerging industries, accepted this arrangement since import tariffs essentially served a purpose. Thus, an economic ceasefire of sorts was established, albeit with stability.

While economic concerns dominated the Convention, the divisive issue of slavery was impossible to ignore. Nevertheless, the issue of slavery—America's sin—cast a long and contentious shadow over these economic discussions. Southern states were deeply concerned that the new federal power might seek to abolish slavery and dismantle their system. Consequently, they insisted that the Constitution explicitly protect slavery. This led to one of the notorious compromises made during the Convention: the Three-Fifths Compromise. Under this agreement, an enslaved person was counted as three-fifths of a person for taxation and representation purposes.

This "compromise" engraved within the Constitution highlighted the painful contradiction at the core of our new nation: a country that proclaimed equality for all men while simultaneously deeming a group of people less than fully human. It was a contradiction that would simmer within American society—a lingering wound destined to erupt into bloody conflict in later decades. The Constitution was the essential fuel to keep the engines running. The discussions revolved around representation, commerce, and sovereignty but ultimately were driven by the goal of securing prosperity. The framers were not merely constructing a nation; they were embarking on an experiment in republican governance at a large scale. They understood that its survival depended on achieving success.

Hamilton's Economic Vision and the Birth of the American Economy

With his financial expertise, Hamilton deeply understood this crucial aspect. As the Secretary of the Treasury, he would go on to develop a comprehensive financial plan that included establishing the First Bank of the United States, creating a national mint, and implementing federal tariffs and excise taxes to repay war debts. These measures aimed to stabilize the young nations' finances and establish America's credibility and economic standing on an international level.

When signing the Constitution, delegates were keenly aware of its imperfections. It was a collection of compromises rather than a fully polished structure. While it contained concessions from both sides to ensure its adoption, numerous details were left for future generations to address and refine. The crafting of the Constitution took into account both economic needs and a long-term vision for a prosperous and united nation. The framers knew that the decisions made during that summer in Philadelphia would have far-reaching effects, impacting future generations. They understood the challenges ahead but remained steadfast in their belief in America's potential. With the Constitution now in place, the real work of building the nation's economic foundation began.

After the signing of the United States Constitution on September 17, 1787, the country's economic story was far from over. It marked the beginning of a chapter as a constitutional republic, where efforts were immediately directed towards addressing war debts, establishing credit, and building a cohesive economy capable of supporting the ambitious American experiment.

After the states joined forces under a central authority, they faced the daunting challenge of building trust among themselves. Imagine a team of rivals, each with their own strategies, suddenly asked to play as one. Trust wasn't available, and economic policies became the battleground on which trust was painstakingly established.

As the First Bank of the United States drew inspiration from the Bank of England, a national currency began circulating within the economy, providing stability in financial matters. The bank became an institution of its time, symbolizing federal strength in economic affairs and acting as a magnet for investments. However, critics such as Thomas Jefferson worried that it granted power to the federal government and favored wealthy city dwellers over average farmers. These debates reflected the enduring struggle between state authority and American society.

Another brainchild of Hamilton was implemented through the Tariff of 1789, which imposed taxes on imported goods and unintentionally stimulated industries. While protective, these tariffs also ignited tensions with trading partners and within boundaries, particularly among those residing in agricultural regions such as the South.

Finding the balance between protecting emerging industries and fostering international trade relationships was a delicate tightrope that the young nation learned to navigate with extreme caution. The Whiskey Rebellion in 1794 served as a test of the federal laws. The government imposed an excise tax on whiskey, which angered frontier distillers. They rose in protest, expressing their opposition to what they saw as excessive government interference. President Washington's decision to personally lead the militia and quell the rebellion became a moment demonstrating the government's determination and capability to enforce its laws, which marked a significant departure from the weak days under the Articles of Confederation.

These economic policies laid the foundation for a country grappling with its identity, torn between simplicity and urban industrial promises. The choices made during those years were not mere policy decisions; they were crucial stepping stones that paved the way for the profound growth of deep divisions and ultimately propelled the United States into becoming a global economic powerhouse.

6

The Political and Ideological Foundations of Early America (1789–1820)

Federalism, Opposition, and Influence on Indigenous and African American Communities 1789–1800

"The Bill of Rights"

Picture a canvas still drying with the vibrant colors of freedom and Revolution. This was how America looked when the presidency began in 1789, with revolutionary leader George Washington as its embodiment. One artist didn't paint this canvas; it was a symphony of brushstrokes. Some are in harmony, others discordant. All crucial to creating the magnificent masterpiece of early American federalism.

Federalism is a system where power is divided between a central authority and local political units. It wasn't a completely new idea, but America added its unique touch to its implementation.

The printed Constitution served as the guiding rulebook, but it was in the hands of leaders like Washington, Adams, Jefferson, and Madison to shape its strategies. These Founding Fathers had diverse perspectives. While Washington was cautious about partisanship, he leaned toward Federalist tendencies and supported a strong central government. Alexander Hamilton, his trusted ally, played a role in establishing a unified economic system that aimed to connect states through shared financial and commercial interests. A nation where your money holds value, whether in the misty ports of Boston or the sun-drenched plantations of Virginia. Hamilton envisioned an America where unity was both valued and practiced.

In opposition were the Democratic-Republicans, led by Thomas Jefferson and James Madison. They celebrated an ideal emphasizing the peaceful harmony of rural life as opposed to Hamilton's industrial vision. To them, America's core resided in its land, with farmers' self-sufficiency and state autonomy at its heart. They viewed the growing federal power with suspicion, fearing that the shadow of tyranny they had escaped might extend its reach into their newfound territory.

The Bill of Rights, which consists of the ten amendments to the Constitution, emerged as a harmonious declaration amid various ideological perspectives. It was officially ratified in 1791. It symbolized America's commitment to protecting the individual freedoms of its citizens and the powers reserved for its states. Rather than viewing it solely as a legal document, it should be seen as a societal agreement—a promise that America would be a place where every person, from farmers to blacksmiths to seamstresses, would have their rights respected just as much as those belonging to the wealthiest plantation or manor owners.

In addition, we must also consider those excluded from these written safeguards—indigenous peoples and enslaved Africans. In these instances, a darker narrative unfolds. The Indian Trade and Intercourse Acts were ostensibly meant to regulate trade and establish boundaries but often infringed upon sovereignty. The numerous treaties, such as those at Fort Harmar in 1789, proved unstable and prone to reinterpretation or outright disregard. The nation's desire for expansion often took precedence over promises made with more genuine intentions.

For enslaved African Americans during this period, little consolation was offered. The Constitution deliberately avoided confronting slavery and included compromises, like the Three-Fifths Compromise. The Fugitive Slave Act of 1793 had an impact, casting a long dark shadow that extended even into states where slavery was abolished. This meant that the stain of bondage could reach places where it shouldn't have existed. As a result, the notion of freedom remained incomplete, contradicting the ideals expressed in important documents and speeches.

Despite these challenges and contradictions, America was in a phase of learning, growth, and self-discovery. Like a child taking their steps, sometimes stumbling but always getting back up with eyes full of hope for what lies ahead.

Federalism

The horizon of the formed republic represented more than just the meeting point of Earth and sky; it symbolized the future and all its possibilities. Unfortunately for people, this horizon often brought clouds of conflict and struggle.

This woven tapestry was now being integrated into the growing quilt of the United States, a process filled with challenges and injustices. It is impossible to discuss this period without acknowledging the impact of the Northwest Indian War (1785-1795), a testament to the unwavering resistance of indigenous peoples. Led by warriors like Little Turtle from the Miami tribe and Blue Jacket from the Shawnees, Native American confederacies east of the Mississippi fought fiercely to protect their ancestral lands from American encroachment. Their battle went beyond military campaigns; it was a fight for their identity and their right to exist on lands that held deep connections to their ancestor's footsteps. The Battle of Fallen Timbers in 1794 became a charged climax, ultimately leading to a problematic resolution with the Treaty of Greenville (1795), which resulted in vast portions of indigenous land being ceded to the U.S. Government.

Let us consider things from a perspective; every piece of land relinquished, and every treaty signed represented a transaction involving soil and grass and a surrendering of memories, histories, and sacred spaces. However, amidst these trials and tribulations, indigenous nations demonstrated an unyielding spirit; they adapted, resisted, and persistently insisted on their place within the larger American narrative.

Running parallel to this struggle was another narrative: that of African Americans. While the voices advocating for freedom were loud, they were somewhat subdued in the plantations and slave quarters. Nonetheless, African Americans did not simply accept their fate within this backdrop. They actively resisted quietly and sometimes with great force. In 1791, the Haitian Revolution began in a French colony, igniting a slave uprising that had far-reaching effects on colonialism in the Western Hemisphere. Despite being miles away, it sparked both hope and fear in America. Hope for those who were enslaved and fear for those who held them captive.

During this time, there was also a flourishing of African-American communities, particularly in Northern states. These communities became centers of activism where free black men and women established schools, churches, and benevolent societies despite the threat posed by the Fugitive Slave Act. They survived and thrived amidst adversity by creating spaces celebrating culture, education, and communal solidarity.

Meanwhile, the federal government grappled with these issues. The Constitution served as a guiding principle. Yet, it also became a source of contention. It contained clauses indirectly referencing slavery that allowed its continuation while pro-claiming liberty for all. The tensions between states' rights and federal power remained unresolved. Tensions often simmered dangerously close to boiling over. To maintain harmony, the government often faced a balancing act, trying to please the slave-holding states in the South while upholding the core principles of the republic. The early days of America were a patchwork creation, not neat and sometimes done hastily. Although, the United States found its essence through forming an identity, asserting sovereignty, and building a sense of community.

As we approached the end of the century, America stood at a crucial juncture where diverse people, cultures, and ideologies competed for a place in shaping the nation's story. Think of America as a stage where multiple plays unfolded simultaneously. Each actor follows their script but together contributes to one epic drama.

the Alien and Sedition Acts of 1798

To illustrate this point, let's consider the Alien and Sedition Acts of 1798. These were not just documents; they played significant roles in this unfolding drama by revealing the young government's fears and desire for control.

Enacted by the Federalists, these laws granted the authority to deport noncitizens deemed "dangerous" and imposed voting requirements on new immigrants. Additionally, they criminalized any form of criticism against the government. Just imagine this scenario: a nation born out of dissent is now suppressing it, a nation built by immigrants now regarding newcomers with suspicion. However, these Acts didn't solely focus on targeting individuals; they also silenced American voices of opposition, particularly those aligned with the Democratic-Republicans, and indirectly impacted various minority communities.

Yet it wasn't lawmakers who shaped America's narrative; its people played a crucial role, too. The Kentucky and Virginia Resolutions, drafted confidentially by Jefferson and Madison in response to the Alien and Sedition Acts, championed states' rights and nullification. These resolutions argued that states could reject laws they considered unconstitutional. This clash represented the essence of federalism, an ongoing power struggle between state and federal governments—a dance that still echoes through history centuries later.

The conclusion of the 1700s marked more than a change in dates; it signified the end of one act in America's story as its characters prepared for what lay ahead. Establishing the nation's two-party system, where Federalists and Democratic-Republicans clashed, served as a precedent for the lively and often tumultuous political discussions that would characterize future American politics. Despite enduring conflicts and broken treaties, Indigenous nations continued to shape American history through their resistance and insistence on maintaining their cultures and identities. African Americans, whether enslaved or free, continued to assert their agency and preserve their culture, leaving a mark on the nation's narrative.

This sets the stage for what comes: an era characterized by expansion and turmoil, innovation and reform—a period that would put the very fabric of national unity to the test. As we lift the curtain on the 1800s, new characters will enter while fresh plots unfold before our eyes. The drama of America's adventure will continue with all its messiness and vibrant glory.

The Jeffersonian and Its Philosophical Foundations 1801–1820

Thomas Jefferson philosophy

As the 19th century began, a new phase unfolded in the United States shaped by a man who would become synonymous with an era: Thomas Jefferson. Envision America as a ship venturing into waters with Jefferson as its captain—a leader with a vision for the republic who firmly believed in an "Empire of Liberty".

Jefferson's rise to the presidency in 1801, referred to as the "Revolution of 1800" marked a shift in American politics. It was more than a change in leadership; it represented a peaceful power transfer between opposing parties—a testament to the nation's growing stability. Picture this: following an election, power transitioned without violence or conflict—an understated acknowledgment of the republic's resilience.

Who was this man, the philosopher-statesman guiding the course of the republic? Jefferson was a figure, a true Renaissance man with a wide range of knowledge and talents. He firmly believed in republicanism, the belief that the destiny of a nation should be determined by its citizens rather than being controlled by a distant monarch or an overpowering aristocracy. He passionately advocated for a society envisioning America as an idyllic landscape sustained by virtuous and independent farmers. Conceive a country with rolling fields instead of polluted factories, where plows and sickles are favored over gears and wheels. This romanticized vision resonated with Americans but overshadowed the harsh realities of slavery and the displacement of indigenous people upon which our nation was built.

Imaginative illustration of Thomas Jefferson's Inauguration

Jefferson's philosophy greatly influenced his policies, including one notable example. The Louisiana Purchase in 1803. This transaction effectively doubled the size of the United States overnight. Picture a canvas of land stretching from New Orleans to the Rocky Mountains, eagerly awaiting to be woven into the tapestry of our nation. However, this acquisition wasn't about gaining territory; it held deep philosophical significance for Jefferson. He saw it as an opportunity for his agrarian ideal to thrive and expand – creating room for his empire of liberty.

The expansion of these lands had a different impact on the indigenous peoples who lived there. It represented a disheartening loss and displacement to them than the liberating waves that Jefferson had envisioned.

It is fascinating to note that Jefferson's life was filled with contradictions despite his promotion of liberty. Take Monticello his estate in Virginia, for example. It served as a microcosm of these paradoxes. Imagine this: a mansion, designed by Jefferson himself, situated atop a hill surrounded by gardens and fields. At the same time, it was also home to enslaved individuals. A stark contrast to the ideals of liberty that he advocated for. In this place where natural beauty coexisted with bondage, the complexities of America's story were laid bare.

Jefferson's time as president merely marked the beginning of an era characterized by dynamism and turbulence. As we delve deeper into this period, we will encounter voices of resistance and moments of transformation that challenged not only Jefferson's vision but also shaped the trajectory of our nation. America's fabric was woven through patterns where conflicts and aspirations intertwined.

Let's get back in time to explore the events, policies, and societal impact during Jefferson's presidency. We will delve into the moments when Jefferson's visions and strategies intersected with the realities of politics, international relations, and human rights. As our narrative unfolds, we witness America grappling with its identity, values, and the essence of freedom.

One pivotal moment during Jefferson's presidency was marked by the Embargo Act of 1807. Picture America as a merchant striving to establish a place in the turbulent global trade markets. Moreover, it was caught between two quarreling giants: Britain and France. In a move, Jefferson implemented the Embargo Act to assert American authority by halting all trade with foreign nations.

Envision this scene: docks eerily silent and empty ships anchored without destinations, in sight goods accumulating in warehouses. Of compelling Europe to respect American neutrality as intended, the Embargo Act ended up backfiring spectacularly. It impacted the American economy, particularly in New England, which heavily relied on commerce and sparked widespread protest. This exemplified how well-intentioned ideas can lead to unintended consequences, highlighting the gap between lofty ideals and practical outcomes.

Mistakes did not solely mark the era. One of its highlights was the Lewis and Clark expedition (1804- 1806), an extraordinary journey commissioned by Jefferson himself. It captivated the nation like an enthralling adventure story as they ventured into uncharted territories, encountering diverse landscapes, cultures, and unprecedented challenges for Euro-Americans.

Even amidst this grand adventure, there were darker aspects. Lewis and Clark's "discovery" meant upheaval and dispossession for nations. The exploratory narrative represented for them the beginning of a tale of loss—a reminder that every story has perspectives and every frontier is someone's home.

As Jefferson's presidency neared its end, it set the stage for new personalities and conflicts to emerge. The tensions during his time as president represented the struggles that continued to shape the nation's path, balancing ideals with realities and different views on liberty and progress. Society was becoming more intricate at the time, with women's voices gaining prominence despite being overlooked in official narratives. Although women like Abigail Adams, who famously urged her husband John Adams to "remember the ladies" and Mercy Otis Warren, a writer and propagandist during the Revolution, were still far from having equal political and social standing as men, they asserted their intellectual and moral authority.

Religious freedom was also changing the Jeffersonian era. While Jefferson's statute on freedom set a precedent, it was through individuals' lived experiences that the nation's commitment to this principle was truly tested. Picture the crowds. Protestants, Catholics, and Jews, among others. Each seeking their place in this 'Empire of Liberty.' Their stories are intricately intertwined within this tapestry of early American life.

Contradictions of an Era

One cannot recount this era without acknowledging the people who lived in the shadows of declarations proclaiming equality for all. Jefferson was contradictory; he wrote the Declaration of Independence, championing the idea that "all men are created equal," yet he owned hundreds of enslaved individuals throughout his lifetime. This contradiction mirrored a nation that was torn within itself in ways.

The Jeffersonian era also witnessed cultural upheaval. New ideas regarding education, religion, and human rights were taking hold. Jefferson, an advocate for education, established the University of Virginia to create a secular institution free from religious influence. This was a move during a time when higher education was primarily associated with religious institutions. Picture young minds eagerly seeking knowledge coming together in the village designed by Jefferson. It was a place where they were encouraged to question, engage in debates, and nurture their dreams.

During this era, there was a surge of creativity in the arts and literature. While European cultural movements impacted American artists and writers, distinctly American voices emerged in their perspectives and experiences. Figures like Washington Irving brought landscapes and legends to life through their writings, captivating the nation's imagination.

Beneath these advancements and idealism lay the reality the land's original inhabitants faced. Native Americans continued to endure displacement and devastation during this period. Under the Jefferson administration, the "civilization program" aimed to assimilate American tribes into Euro-American agricultural practices and social norms. Unfortunately, this policy eroded cultures and ways of life over time. It was a moving tragedy disguised as benevolence and progress – a poignant reminder that history often crushes those caught in its path.

Reflecting on the Jeffersonian era, we witness a nation that experienced growth and transformation. Carries within it deep-rooted contradictions and conflicts. The concepts of freedom, democracy, and the national path will continue to unfold, with new individuals taking center stage, each influenced by the legacies. Both negative. Of this pivotal period in American history.

Jefferson's presidency initiated dynamics that would shape the character and destiny of the country. The westward expansion, the entrenchment of slavery as a system, the displacement of peoples, and the flourishing of a distinct national culture were all integral elements interwoven into the fabric of American history during this time. These elements would continue to entangle generations in discussions about the essence and course of the nation.

American Economy, Technological Progress, and Environmental Factors Segment

Foundations of America's Economic Advancements

As the 19th century began, the United States stood as a nation brimming with immense potential. Our story now takes us through the streets of early American cities and the vast, untamed frontiers, delving into the core elements that shaped this growing country – its economy, technological innovations, and the boundless environment that nurtured and presented challenges to its people.

The American economy is like a young sapling weathering a turbulent climate. The aftermath of the Revolutionary War had left this nation economically vulnerable. British blockades had disrupted trade routes while domestic industries were still in infancy. However, amidst these hardships emerged a spirit of resilience and ingenuity among Americans that sowed seeds that would later fuel their economic prowess.

Agriculture formed the backbone of America's economy during this era, with farmers playing a crucial role. Nevertheless, it wasn't only corn and wheat swaying in the breeze; cash crops like cotton and tobacco played roles in this agricultural tale, especially in the Southern states. Imagine the cotton fields stretching out like oceans under the sun with the air filled with the sounds of hard work. In these rows of growth, both the wealth of nations and the profound suffering of enslaved individuals coexisted, casting a long shadow over economic prosperity.

As we move towards the north, the landscape transforms. The clamor and noise of a burgeoning sector drown out nature's harmonies. The late 18th and 19th centuries marked America's entry into the Industrial Revolution. It was a period characterized by thrilling inventions and formidable mills and factories. Picture those textile mills emerging along rivers, their water wheels spinning vigorously to power looms that wove together the fabric of a modern economy.

What primarily fueled these looms, mills, and overall progress? It was cotton. Here lies an intertwined narrative linking industrial strength with Southern agriculture through the thread of cotton production while underpinned by slavery's sad reality.

It is also crucial to spotlight the overlooked individuals who played a vital role in driving progress: the skilled artisans and hardworking laborers. They were the economy's lifeblood, working tirelessly to support growing commerce and infrastructure. Their efforts powered projects like building canals and roads connecting distant communities and markets.

While we admire the ingenuity that fueled economic growth, let us not forget to focus on the vast American environment that nurtured this emerging nation. The land was both generous and challenging, playing a significant role in shaping America's story. It provided soils for farming and mighty rivers that facilitated trade and transportation but posed formidable obstacles.

The wilderness of the New World was a mix of awe-inspiring wonders and constant threats, forcing its inhabitants to adapt to nature's whims continually. Early Americans were not merely settlers; they were negotiators engaged in a dialogue with their surroundings. They faced weather patterns capable of blessing one harvest season while devastating the next. Additionally, they explored territories that promised both wealth and danger simultaneously. The scene is set with all the elements of America's economic and technological identity in place. The environment plays both a supporting role and a challenging adversary. Yet, as progress unfolds, new ideas, inventions, and obstacles loom on the horizon.

Now, let's delve into the heart of innovation and its many implications. The United States in the 1800s is something like a bustling workshop buzzing with inventive sparks. Each new idea ignites the flames of change. One significant invention that stands out is Eli Whitney's cotton gin. Created in 1793, this machine revolutionized cotton production. Left behind a complex legacy. While it dramatically reduced the labor required for cleaning cotton, it also reinforced the reliance on plantation slavery, further entangling the nation in an issue that would persist for many years. In these moments of innovation and brilliance, we witness the interplay between progress and ethics, a recurring theme throughout American history. In the exhilarating rush of embracing possibilities, our nation often surged ahead without fully considering the moral consequences accompanying such advancements.

In the realm of transportation, we encounter a figure: Robert Fulton. Just guess the wonderment of spectators as Fulton's steamboat, the Clermont, embarked on its inaugural journey up the Hudson River in 1807. The steamboat was more than an invention; it symbolized a transformation in how we perceived space and time—a precursor to our vision of an interconnected United States. With steam power at its helm, goods, ideas, and people could move more than ever, drawing our vast country closer together into a more vibrant whole.

This tapestry of technology was not without its imperfections. As canals and roads snaked across our landscape—forests being cleared and wilderness being tamed—it showcased humanity's spirit and a gentle reminder that we were teetering on a delicate balance. The environment itself was abundant and forgiving but not infinite; enough signs of exploitation began to surface.

It wasn't just the land that endured these costs. The growing factories represented progress and were both places of opportunity and exploitation. Men, women, and even children often worked hours in terrible conditions. The factory whistle dictated their lives, and the repetitive sound of machinery acted as both a soothing lullaby and a constant supervisor.

Acknowledging the contributions of those whose stories have been overlooked during this period is essential. Nonetheless, enslaved African Americans were not merely passive observers during these times. Skilled artisans like blacksmiths, carpenters, and other experts emerged from their ranks. Their forced expertise played a role in shaping the American economy. Similarly, Native American communities faced the surge of expansion with resilience and practicality. Some adopted farming methods, while others navigated the emerging capitalist economy while maintaining a deep spiritual and cultural connection to their ancestral lands.

As we conclude, this segment lets us reflect on the contradictions that early Americans grappled with daily. They reached for the future with one hand while often turning a blind eye to its consequences with the other. They were inventors, workers, visionaries, and survivors. They constructed an economic machine that would drive a global superpower, but unfortunately, it often relied on the hard work and suffering of those who had no power or rights.

The stage for America's story is set, with all the key players ready. As this act begins, the narrative unfolds. So, please don't leave your seats because the story is far from its conclusion. The journey of progress with its successes and challenges is about to unfold in the chapters.

Human lives

Let's draw back the curtain on the lives affected as our story unravels. Sometimes abruptly. By this whirlwind of economic growth and technological advancement. Imagine a family like The Millers residing in a farmhouse in rural Pennsylvania during the early 1800s. With the beginning of that century came changes to alter their lives along with others. One of the children in the Miller family, inspired by the tales of Eli Whitney, would spend time tinkering in their barn, dreaming of inventing something. Upon hearing stories of spinning jennies and water frames in factories, their daughter would long for the freedom and excitement of working in a bustling mill town. However, the parents, who have experienced years of work on the land, might hold reservations towards these new contraptions—a sentiment shared by many families.

The innovations during that era weren't technological advancements; they had profound social implications that reshaped families, communities, and societal norms. The factory system enticed workers to leave life behind with promises of stable income but at the expense of long hours and little concern for human well-being. The clear line between home and work blurred as factory life set a pace that became accepted as usual.

Nevertheless, amidst all this turmoil, the indomitable human spirit flourished. Workers began organizing themselves secretly and then openly; their collective voice grew more assertive. These early struggles laid down the roots for a labor movement that would eventually champion the rights and dignity of working-class individuals.

Let us not overlook another player in our story: the environment silently observing these events unfold. As pioneers expanded westward, motivated by government policies and the promise of prosperity, the magnificent scenery of America transformed. Forests retreated as axes advanced, and plains were cultivated under the eye of farmers. Native species of plants and animals faced challenges, with some becoming extinct before they could be thoroughly documented by science.

Amidst this narrative of exploitation, there were also whispers of harmony and respect. Though facing difficulties, Indigenous communities presented ways of interacting with nature, not as something to conquer but as a sacred responsibility to protect. Their voices may have been overshadowed during that era's chaos, but they carry an enduring message that still reverberates in today's environmental conversations.

The tale of America is not only carved into its majestic mountains and winding rivers but also woven into the dreams and hard work of its citizens. It's a dance between progress and heritage, growth and preservation.

The Impact of Science and Technology on American Life

Science and technology during the early years

In our tale of America's history, science and technology emerge as quiet revolutionaries, subtly sparking change and reshaping everyday existence. Picture a world where candles and oil lamps push back the darkness, measuring distance takes weeks or months, and the mysteries of the universe are pondered through philosophy and religious beliefs. This was America and much of the world as the 18th century ended. With each passing day, progress began to unfold.

Enter Benjamin Franklin, a man whose name would soon be synonymous with curiosity in the hearts of Americans. Imagine him standing with a kite in hand, daring to challenge the heavens themselves in his quest to unravel the secrets behind lightning.

Franklin's experiments with electricity went beyond daring acts; they represented a growing thirst for knowledge, a boldness that challenged the unknown instead of fearing it. Nonetheless, science encompassed more than grand experiments. It involved the seeds of change in life. Consider the impact of vaccination, which became accessible to the public during this era following Edward Jenner's groundbreaking work with the smallpox vaccine. Communities devastated by diseases, lives cut short soon, and families torn apart by illness. Then, amidst this gloomy picture emerges a ray of hope: the possibility of prevention and protection. Vaccination campaigns initially faced skepticism and fear, reflecting humanity's resistance to what is new and unfamiliar. Nevertheless, they. Saved countless lives, showcasing the enduring power of scientific progress.

Changes also brewed within households. The Franklin stove, an invention by our polymath Benjamin Franklin, revolutionized home heating. It was more than an appliance; it represented a promise of warmth, reduced firewood consumption, and families huddled together in winter, sharing stories while their laughter defied the howling wind outside. In these yet intimate moments, we witness the genuine face of technological advancement.

However, it wasn't all sunshine and happiness during this time. The turn of the century also created a dilemma regarding science and technology. Slavery, which was already a stain on the conscience of our nation, found an ally in technology. The invention of the cotton gin, originally intended to reduce labor, ended up increasing the demand for slave labor and perpetuating this cruel institution. This serves as a reminder that scientific progress cannot exist without moral considerations, and every step forward requires carefully examining its impact on society.

Growing industries

As our story unfolds, we witness a nation on the brink of embracing modernity. When out at sea, the stars were not beautiful twinkling lights in the night sky; they served as guiding beacons, silent guardians determining the destiny of ships and their crews. During this time, sailors relied on a tool called a sextant to navigate with unprecedented accuracy. Picture a captain standing on the swaying deck of his ship, feeling the mist of salt spray on his face as he peers through his sextant, carefully calculating and recalculating, fully aware that the fate of his entire vessel rests upon the precise alignment of celestial bodies.

This era also marked the stages of industrialization in America. The progress was accompanied by a rhythm—a symphony characterized by the clattering sounds emanating from spinning jennies and looms. The first factories emerged, forever changing the landscape of work and livelihoods. Picture yourself in those pioneering mills in New England—the air with raw cotton and wool scents and faint vibrations reverberating through the ground from ceaselessly moving machinery. Within these revered halls of industry, a new American dream began to take shape—a vision of prosperity fueled by technological advancements.

Furthermore, it is crucial to balance the idealized perceptions of this industrial activity with the harsh realities of that era. The advent of the factory system brought about a side of exploitation and hardship. Workers, including women and children, endured hours in often terrible conditions. Nevertheless, amidst this backdrop was a glimmer of resilience and camaraderie. Workers shared struggles and small moments of joy in their lives, reflecting the endurance of spirit in the face of relentless industrial ambition.

The realm of communication was not left untouched by the winds of change either. The invention of the telegraph by Samuel Morse in 1837, although later in the 19th century, foreshadowed a future interconnected society. DO you see the awe?-the inspiring experience of sending messages across distances within minutes instead of weeks or months! It effectively shrank our nation in operational terms, weaving together its various parts with each dispatched telegram.

Scientific pursuits were also on a quest during this period, witnessing the emergence and evolution of new disciplines. For instance, paleontology—a field ignited by the discovery of ancient bones- compelled humanity to question life's origins on Earth deeply. Let's take a moment to reflect on the progress made in medicine. We have come away from relying on humour and leeches to having a more sophisticated understanding of human health, although still not as advanced as today's standards.

Pushing boundaries

Moving forward in our journey, we must acknowledge that scientific and technological breakthroughs during this period didn't just alter Americans' actions; they fundamentally trans-formed their thoughts, aspirations, and even their sense of self. The American spirit of "can do" wasn't born out of thin air; it emerged from a crucible shaped by innovation and exploration. Let's take a look at education, for example. In the 1700s and early 1800s, America wasn't yet the center of an educational revolution. The seeds of change were already being planted. With the rise of newspapers and the establishment of libraries, information became more accessible to people from all walks of life. This created a thirst for knowledge that went beyond class and wealth. Imagine a farm worker with hands still stained from hard labor reading a newspaper and dreaming about worlds beyond his own.

It's important to remember women's contributions during this era, even though they are often overlooked in scientific and technological progress discussions. Women faced obstacles when it came to education during this period. Yet, some brave individuals defied norms and fought for their right to learn. One such inspiring figure was Emma Willard, who advocated for women's education by establishing schools. She understood that knowledge should be accessible to everyone regardless of gender.

While these shifts were happening within society, physical changes occurred across the nation's landscape. Infrastructure took center stage with projects like the construction of the Erie Canal, which was completed in 1825 (a bit outside our current timeline but relevant to our discussion). The human effort that went into such a monumental endeavor. They transformed the landscape into a waterway connecting goods, people, and ideas in previously unseen ways.

In contrast, this growth came with its set of consequences.

The expanding agriculture and industry had an often ignored impact on the environment. Forests were cut down relentlessly. The air became polluted with industrial smoke. The perspective was that nature, with all its beauty and wonder, was merely a resource to be controlled and utilized. This mindset laid the foundation for conservation movements that would fight to preserve America's natural wonders for many generations.

What about the people? How did they perceive these whirlwinds of change? For some, it was an era of opportunities where the American Dream shone brightly, like a path illuminated by stars. However, for others marginalized or excluded from society, progress only reminded them of the barriers preventing their access to prosperity.

Now, let's envision America as a nation standing on the edge. In front lies an expansive future, while behind are memories of darkness and light from its days. The decisions taken in this era, the aspirations pursued, and the obstacles overcome all shaped the intricate fabric of a nation's character. This laid the foundation for the transformative years that lay ahead.

IV

ANTEBELLUM, CIVIL WAR, AND RECONSTRUCTION

7

Society Tensions and Changes
(1820–1877)

Antebellum Society, Women's Roles and Social Transformations 1820–1850

Women's changing roles and perceptions

The Antebellum era in America, which existed before the Civil War, is often seen as a time of conflict and societal divisions. However, it was also a period of cultural, economic, and social changes. Within this context, women's roles underwent transformations that challenged norms and had a subtle yet influential impact on shaping the nation's trajectory.

In the 1820s, America was such a country cherishing its hard-fought independence while grappling with political disagreements and economic fluctuations. Now, let us zoom in on women's experiences during this time. In the past, it was common to see women depicted in traditional roles, confined to domestic life. Yet, this only scratches the surface of a much deeper and more turbulent reality.

During the Antebellum period, some women defied societal limitations and started to bring about change. One area where they made progress was in education. While most educational institutions were dominated by men, the early 19th century witnessed a rise in seminaries and academies. Emma Willard's Troy Female Seminary, established in 1821 in New York, stood out as a shining example. Willard advocated for women's education and firmly believed in their intellectual equality. Her seminary went beyond teaching domestic skills expected of women and delved into subjects like mathematics, philosophy, and science – previously considered beyond women's capabilities.

Now we must ask ourselves: why was education crucial? It's like a key – a key that unlocked the chains of confinement and allowed women to step into new roles that were previously unimaginable. Educated women began to enter the public realm not all at once like an overwhelming flood but rather like a persistent flow that slowly eroded the rigid societal structures.

As we continue our exploration of the Antebellum period, we will encounter women who used their writing as a form of resistance to challenging societal norms through literature and journalism. We will follow the journey of abolitionists, suffragists, and social reformers who dared to envision a world where equality was paramount. We must delve into women's lives from various social and economic backgrounds, including those often overlooked enslaved individuals and indigenous women.

During this era of transformation, the idea of the "cult of domesticity" emerged. This ideology confined women to their homes, portraying them as pure and submissive beings. Yet, women found ways to exert power and influence within these restrictive expectations. Join me in uncovering the truths behind the Antebellum stage. Together, we will unveil the often surprising ways women challenged traditions and played a pivotal role in shaping American society.

"Woman in the Nineteenth Century"

Let's uncover women's lives, such as Margaret Fuller, Harriet Beecher Stowe, and Sojourner Truth. Each was a powerhouse in her own right, using their pens to champion important causes. Fuller, an author, editor, and critic, championed women's rights in America. Her book "Woman in the Nineteenth Century" (1845) is recognized as a feminist work that challenged patriarchal norms at that time.

Think of the courage it took for Fuller to raise her voice during an era when expectations dominated by men often silenced such voices. Let's talk about Harriet Beecher Stowe, who made an impact with her renowned work "Uncle Tom's Cabin". This novel, published in 1852, went beyond storytelling; it managed to humanize enslaved individuals and expose the cruelties of slavery to those who had previously been indifferent. It is even said that this book played a part in starting a war. Imagine reading a book in the comfort of your home as it gently unravels your prejudices and forces you to acknowledge the humanity you had previously overlooked.

On the other hand, Sojourner Truth stands as a symbol of resilience. Born into slavery but managing to escape and find freedom, her life became an inspiration for women. She didn't just express herself through writing; she roared with conviction in her speech titled "Ain't I a Woman?" Her words echoed through women's conventions and left an indelible mark on history. Truth passionately advocated for suffrage and equality, becoming a strong voice for women's rights and the anti-slavery movement.

Conversely, we must recognize that progress during the Antebellum era was far from straightforward. While some women were writing literature, others faced harsh realities within the confines of their lives. Enslaved women endured horrors often overshadowed by larger narratives. We mustn't forget the factory workers, the unsung heroes toiling in dangerous conditions for meager wages, instrumental in the progress of industrialization.

The movements advocating for women's suffrage were also gaining momentum, with influential figures like Elizabeth Cady Stanton and Susan B. Anthony paving the way despite facing opposition. The Seneca Falls Convention of 1848 marked an occasion—a collective outcry for women's rights. It was more than a gathering; it was a resounding call that resonated through the years, igniting a flame carried by future generations.

In this mix of progress and hardship, society struggled with contradictions. The notion of the "cult of domesticity" still prevailed, dictating that women should be guardians confined to their homes even as more women began participating in public life. These intricate dynamics set the stage for the Civil War, with societal tensions foreshadowing upheaval on various fronts.

Different racial and social backgrounds

As we delve deeper into the story of Antebellum society, it becomes increasingly evident that women's experiences were as varied as the nation itself. This period was defined not only by prominent voices that resonated loudly but also by those whose voices were suppressed yet resilient in their pursuit of recognition and rights.

Let us now turn our attention to the unsung women, those often overlooked in history books yet who were foundational to society. In the states, African American women held in slavery endured unimaginable hardships. Yet, their stories weren't tales of sorrow; they were narratives of resilience and perseverance in preserving their cultures against attempts at erasure. These women maintained bonds that safeguarded their heritage and, through whispers and songs, kept alive a flicker of hope for freedom.

In contrast, let's consider the experiences of Native American women during the Antebellum period, a time of great turmoil for Native communities. The Indian Removal Act of 1830 forced individuals to leave their ancestral lands, and this journey became marked by both resilience and tragedy, as seen in events like the Trail of Tears. These courageous women, who held the fabric of their communities, found themselves protecting the very essence of their people. Their stories are intertwined with pain. Also, highlight their strength in preserving their heritage, making them an integral part of our nation's narrative.

Amidst these moments, there were also glimpses of hope with the emergence of organized women's labor movements. The Lowell Mill Girls were primarily composed of women working in textile mills during the 1830s. They bravely staged strikes and protests against labor practices and conditions. While they didn't consistently achieve success, their actions signaled a significant shift towards collective protest among female workers—a precursor to later labor movements that would transcend industries and genders.

In parallel, as the women's rights movement began to flourish, it was counterbalanced by restrictions on African American freedom—both for the enslaved and those who had gained their freedom. One such example was the Fugitive Slave Act of 1850, which cast a shadow over free African Americans who now found themselves at risk even after attaining liberty. This division and conflict within the country set the stage for the onset of War. As the 1850s approached their end, the nation was on the verge of conflict. The women during the Antebellum era played roles and had diverse experiences, bringing about visible and yet-to-be-realized changes. Their unique stories became essential to the larger narrative, propelling the nation toward a critical juncture defining its identity and fate.

As we conclude our exploration of the landscape encompassing women's roles in Antebellum society, it becomes clear that these stories were not mere footnotes but integral to comprehending the intricacies of a nation teetering on the edge. Unbeknownst to them, they set in motion a series of events leading to turmoil; their aspirations, challenges, and everyday lives contributed to a crescendo that ultimately found release through wartime tribulations.

Pathways to Conflict: Slavery and Sectionalism: 1851–1860,

The North and the South

The 1850s in America were, in many ways, akin to a theatrical overture, where each section of the orchestra begins to play louder and more passionately, not in harmony but in a clashing crescendo that foreshadows the drama about to unfold. In this decade, the nation wasn't just walking towards division; it was sprinting, with every event acting as a sprinter's stride, propelling it forward more rapidly and irreversibly.

Painting illustration in 19th-century America, where a politician speaks from a wooden platform

Picture America during this time: a nation expanding west-ward under the banner of "Manifest Destiny", yet internally, it was anything but united. The issue? Slavery – an institution as old as America itself, deeply entrenched in the country's economic, cultural, and social foundations, particularly in the South.

The Compromise of 1850, intended as a temporary solution, only highlighted the festering wound beneath. It admitted California as a free state, tipped the balance in the Senate in favor of free states, and enraged the South. Yet, it also included a more stringent Fugitive Slave Law, which was supposed to appease the South but inflamed Northern sentiment against slavery.

Think of the everyday Northerner's horror as the new law required them to be complicit in the sin of slavery. Refusal to participate in the capture of an escaped enslaved person, someone they saw not as property but as a fellow human being seeking freedom, could lead to hefty fines and imprisonment. The streets weren't just avenues in cities; they became moral battlegrounds.

It's during this period that we meet individuals like Harriet Beecher Stowe. Picture her, a woman of small stature but immense resolve, taking the nation's pain and channeling it into "Uncle Tom's Cabin" (1852). Her novel didn't just tell a story; it showed the North the inhumanity of slavery and the South what the North was beginning to stand for. It's said that when Abraham Lincoln met Stowe at the start of the Civil War, he remarked, "So you're the little woman who wrote the book that made this great war!"

Yet, the divide wasn't just moral; it was political. The Kansas-Nebraska Act of 1854, introduced by Senator Stephen A. Douglas, undid the fragile peace maintained by the Missouri Compromise. It allowed settlers in the newly organized territories, without regard to the previous 36°30′ latitude boundary established by the Missouri Compromise, to decide the slavery question by popular sovereignty, potentially opening all future territories to slavery. The result? "Bleeding Kansas" where pro- and anti-slavery settlers flooded Kansas, each side determined to influence the vote. The territory became a microcosm of the national tension, with violent clashes and widespread fraud in voting practices.

In the midst of this, the figure of John Brown emerged, a man whose name would become synonymous with anti-slavery militancy. The Pottawatomie Massacre in 1856, where Brown and his followers killed five pro-slavery settlers in Kansas, marked one of the first times the conflict turned bloody, a precursor of the violence soon to engulf the entire nation. Amidst these events, the fabric of the Union began to fray at an alarming rate, setting the stage for the events of the late 1850s, which would only pull the threads faster and more fiercely.

The Dred Scott decision and the political ascent of Abraham Lincoln

As the 1850s wore on, conflict and strife increasingly authored the American narrative. It was a story written in the rulings of judges, the speeches of politicians, and the blood of its citizens. This period in history wasn't just a chapter in a book; it was a series of explosive episodes, each escalating the drama and tension to unprecedented heights.

In 1857, the United States Supreme Court delivered a decision that can only be described as a seismic shock to an already quaking nation. Dred Scott, an enslaved person who had resided in a free state, filed suit for his freedom on the grounds of his extended stay in free territory. The Court's decision? Not only was Scott still enslaved, but African Americans were not and could never be citizens of the United States. Furthermore, the Court declared the Missouri Compromise unconstitutional, asserting that Congress had no authority to prohibit slavery in the territories.

Picture Dred Scott: a man who sought freedom through the promise of American justice, only to be told he was less than a man in the eyes of the law. His case wasn't just about a legal ruling; it was a manifestation of the disregard for African-American humanity pervasive in society. It sent a clear message to the North: the highest Court in the land saw no issue with the spread of slavery.

As this decision rippled across the nation, the stage was set for the emergence of a figure who would come to symbolize the anti-slavery movement and the Union's struggle during the Civil War: Abraham Lincoln. A country lawyer known for his eloquence and moral stance against slavery, Lincoln wasn't just a politician but a beacon of hope in a storm of chaos.

The Lincoln-Douglas debates of 1858, though focused on the Illinois Senate race, captured the nation's attention and crystallized the divide between the free and enslaved person states. Stephen Douglas, the incumbent, championed popular sovereignty, while Lincoln countered with a moral argument against the spread of slavery. Though Lincoln lost the Senate race, these debates catapulted him onto the national stage and into the heart of the brewing storm.

But this era wasn't just about politics and court decisions; violent confrontations also defined it. The raid on Harpers Ferry in 1859, led by John Brown, was one of the most controversial episodes of the time. Brown and his followers aimed to initiate an armed slave revolt by seizing a federal arsenal. Though the raid was quickly suppressed, and Brown was captured and executed, the incident sent shockwaves throughout the country. Many lauded Brown as a martyr for a noble cause in the North, while the South saw the raid as proof of the North's intent to wage War on the Southern way of life.

Imagine the fear and defiance in the hearts of Southerners as they perceived threats not just to their economic system but to their very lives. Conversely, picture the determination of the North to combat what they viewed as a moral abomination. These weren't just regional attitudes but convictions etched into the identities of all who held them.

As the decade neared its end, the election of 1860 loomed on the horizon. This wasn't just an election; it was a crossroads for a country grappling with its soul, a choice between further division or an attempt at unity through the escalating tension.

Election of 1860

The year 1860 arrived, a year that would end with a fractured nation. The election season was not just a political contest; it was a battle for the future soul of the United States. Picture four candidates, each representing different facets of a splintering country: Abraham Lincoln of the Republican Party, Stephen A. Douglas of the Northern Democrats, John C. Breckinridge of the Southern Democrats, and John Bell of the Constitutional Union Party.

Lincoln, the candidate of the fledgling Republican Party, ran on a platform that opposed the expansion of slavery into the territories. He didn't advocate for immediate abolition — that position was too radical even for many in the North — but his stance was clear: "A house divided against itself cannot stand". This election was like a complex chess match with the nation's destiny hanging in the balance. The Democratic Party was split along sectional lines, and the Southern Democrats, with Breckinridge, supported the protection of slavery in the territories. Douglas, meanwhile, continued to push for popular sovereignty, letting the settlers in each territory decide on slavery. Bell, representing the Constitutional Union Party, sought to avoid secession by ignoring the slavery issue altogether and upholding the Union.

Now, let's contemplate the tension of election night, November 6, 1860. The results came in, and Abraham Lincoln won the presidency without receiving a single electoral vote from the South. He wasn't even on the ballot in most Southern states. This victory, achieved without Southern support, highlighted the deep divisions in the country.

The South viewed Lincoln's election as the final straw. It was one thing to grapple with a distant federal government but quite another to face a President and a growing political force opposed to expanding their way of life. The first to react was South Carolina, seceding from the Union on December 20, 1860. The dominos fell quickly after that, with Mississippi, Florida, Alabama, Georgia, Louisiana, and Texas following suit. Picture this not as a list of states but as a gathering storm, each state's secession another thunderclap echoing across the land. Each ordinance of secession was not just a political document but a declaration that the Union, as it had stood, was irreparably broken. They didn't see it as rebellion but as a defense of their rights and way of life.

The Confederacy was formed in the whirlwind of secession,

and Jefferson Davis was elected president. The stage was set, the actors in place, and the American tragedy was ready to unfold. But the curtain hadn't risen just yet. There was a lull, a breath held, as Lincoln made his way to Washington for his inauguration, traveling through a nation holding its breath.

Lincoln's inaugural address on March 4, 1861, was a plea for unity. He stated that he had no intent to invade Southern states or interfere with slavery where it existed. But he also asserted that no state had the right to break up the Union. The message was clear: secession was not the answer. But for the South, this was a path its leaders felt they had to take, a path they believed led to their survival. As Lincoln settled into office, the storm broke loose, and the shots fired at Fort Sumter on April 12, 1861, were the lightning that lit the sky of a nation at War with itself.

Cultural, Religious, and Economic Factors Leading to the Civil War

Pre-Civil War conditions

To truly grasp the essence of the Civil War, it is crucial to delve into the lives and experiences of its people and comprehend the society they had built. Picture Antebellum America as a captivating mosaic composed of pieces that painted a troubled yet significant image together.

Between 1820 and 1860, the United States experienced a wave of immigration. People embarked on journeys across vast oceans with nothing but hope in their hearts. The Irish population surged onto American shores, primarily fleeing the devastating Potato Famine of the 1840s. Over the 19th century, their numbers in the U.S. grew substantially, with many settling in cities where they played a vital role in the labor force despite often facing discrimination and adversity.

Germans, too, sought solace in America, fleeing from unrest that followed the failed revolutions of 1848. They brought with them their traditions, culture, and valuable skills that greatly enriched the fabric of American society. The lively German communities established breweries, newspapers, and cultural organizations in cities like Milwaukee, St. Louis, and Cincinnati, infusing them with a touch of charm. These immigrant groups, among others, not only transformed the demographic landscape but also profoundly impacted politics, culture, and the economy. However, their arrival was not universally embraced. The emergence of sentiments and groups like the Know Nothings revealed a darker aspect of the American character that was resistant to change and apprehensive towards outsiders.

Religious diversity also experienced growth during the Antebellum era. The Second Great Awakening swept across the nation in the 19th century, leading to denominational divisions and inspiring new religious movements. Visualize vibrant tent revivals filled with preaching and an overwhelming enthusiasm for newfound faith, resulting in social reforms such as temperance advocacy, abolitionism efforts, and women's rights activism. Moreover, there was increased religious diversity, with Catholicism experiencing notable growth, primarily due to Irish immigrants and, to a lesser extent, German immigrants.

Judaism also saw increased establishment as immigrants arrived, mainly from German-speaking regions of Europe. This period witnessed the emergence of new religions, such as the Mormon faith and the Church of Jesus Christ of Latter-day Saints, founded by Joseph Smith in 1830.

This religious diversity reflected American society, a blend of passionate and often conflicting beliefs. Faith influenced aspects of public life, including education and politics, and highlighted deep divisions on slavery and states' rights.

Economic Divergence: The Great Divide

The Antebellum United States was as two economies: the industrious North and the rural South. While they coexisted and depended on each other in some ways, they were fundamentally different. The North was a hub of activity and innovation with its factories, railroads, and growing cities. Immigrants played a role in this economic engine by providing a steady stream of eager workers seeking opportunities.

On the other hand, the Southern economy relied heavily on agriculture—primarily focused on cotton—and was intertwined with slavery. Picture vast plantations adorned with fields of cotton where enslaved individuals toiled; their lives formed the very foundation for this wealth. The invention of the cotton gin by Eli Whitney in 1793 revolutionized cotton production, making cotton cultivation more profitable and thereby further cementing slavery's importance to the Southern economy.

As we delve further into the era of Antebellum America, we encounter a nation struggling to define itself amidst a wave of transformations. This period marked an influx of cultural influences, sincere religious beliefs, and turbulent economic changes. It served as a moment during which the American identity was shaped and put to the test.

Let's take a journey to the cities of Antebellum America, where the streets echoed with a mix of languages and the air was filled with the enticing aromas of cuisines. In this atmosphere, different cultures collided and merged. Theatres, newspapers, and literature flourished, providing an escape from and a commentary on the changing society. Imagine yourself sitting in a New York theatre enjoying a play that humorously pokes fun at the political issues of that time or reading a novel like Harriet Beecher Stowe's "Uncle Tom Cabin" which boldly brought slavery's harsh realities to the forefront of American consciousness.

Not to mention, cultural integration came with its share of challenges. There were often outbreaks of sentiments leading to violence, such as the deadly Philadelphia Nativist Riots in 1844. Legislative actions, such as restrictive immigration laws, sought to control the lives of immigrants, while measures like the Black Codes later aimed to control the lives of free African Americans.

Illustration showing Philadelphia Nativist Riots in 1844

Faith and Morality: The Moral Compass of a Nation

Now, envision gatherings, impassioned speeches, and grass-roots campaigns during this era of numerous reform movements. Religion and morality formed foundations for causes like temperance (opposing alcohol consumption), women's suffrage (fighting for women's right to vote), educational reform, and, most controversially, abolitionism (the movement against slavery). Prominent historical figures such as Frederick Douglass, Sojourner Truth, and William Lloyd Garrison played a role not only as activists but also as the moral compass guiding a nation in search of its core principles of freedom and justice.

The abolitionist movement, while commendable, also brought

about discord. Although many Northerners opposed slavery, not everyone believed in equality or was fully prepared for the societal changes accompanying abolition. In the South, where the economy relied heavily on slavery, some saw the movement threatening their way of life.

The contrasting economies of the North and South were not background settings for societal tensions; they played significant roles in shaping events. The North thrived with its expanding industries, flourishing cities, and growing infrastructure—an embodiment of progress and modernity. Picture bustling textile mills, with clattering machinery steam engines pulling train cars along tracks and canals filled with activity—a reflection of innovation and growth. In contrast, the South remained predominantly rural. Focused on agriculture. Envision cotton fields stretching out before you alongside grand plantation homes—symbols of wealth built upon the labor of enslaved individuals.

As the movement against slavery gained momentum, resistance in the slavery-dependent South grew stronger. Although the economies of the North and South appeared to be vastly different, they were closely intertwined. The South provided cotton to mills, while the North supplied manufactured goods that were in demand in the South. However, this interdependence faced challenges such as tariffs that protected Northern industries but increased costs for Southern states.

As these economic, cultural, and moral forces clashed, it pushed the nation towards a path where finding compromises became increasingly difficult. The Kansas-Nebraska Act of

1854 exemplified this struggle when it allowed territories to decide on slavery and led to violence in "Bleeding Kansas". It made it clear that resolving the issue of slavery would not be achieved through legislative means.

By the 1850s, tensions had reached a breaking point within the United States. The election of Abraham Lincoln posed a perceived threat to Southern states and served as a final straw amidst numerous grievances. Secession became inevitable, exposing rooted wounds within the country and setting the stage for the Civil War.

The Decade of Discord: America's 1860s Dilemma

As the 1860s began in the United States, the nation found itself at a juncture. It struggled with the conflict between its founding ideals and the harsh realities of divisions. Various factors had been pulling at the fabric of society, such as immigration, economic disparities, moral reform movements, and, notably, the contentious issue of slavery. These factors left the country divided and fragile.

Following the Kansas-Nebraska Act, the well-known Second Party System was broken down. The Whigs disintegrated, and divisions arose within the Democrats. In their place emerged the Republican Party with a solid commitment to halting the expansion of slavery. Imagine a time filled with debates, passionate rallies, and fervent election campaigns. All these events revolved around one truth: the issue of slavery had permeated every aspect of political discourse, serving as the ultimate test for all national decisions.

The 1857 Supreme Court ruling in the Dred Scott case shook the nation. This decision declared that African Americans were not citizens with the right to sue, and it stated that Congress had no authority to regulate slavery in the territories. The shockwaves generated by this ruling reverberated throughout the country. Just envision the outrage and passion it ignited. From impassioned speeches and sermons to hushed conversations in lit rooms. All reflective of a nation grappling with its moral conscience.

As the 1860 election approached, anticipation hung heavy in the air. Abraham Lincoln, representing the Republican Party, stood as a symbol of opposition against slavery despite his assurances that he would not interfere with existing slave-holding states. Nevertheless, his victory signaled a perceived decrease in power and influence for Southern states within the Union. It was almost as if a switch had been flipped; what was once a notion. Secession. It became an undeniable reality, starting with the South Carolina Declaration, followed by other Southern states.

Just try to picture Charleston, South Carolina, when its secession convention formally announced the state's break from the Union. The contrasting emotions of individuals reflected the division within the nation. The decision made had an impact resonating throughout the Southern states and leading to similar gatherings. Then, on April 12, 1861, Confederate forces fired the first shots at Fort Sumter. These volleys shattered the morning's tranquility and marked the end of an era known as Antebellum. It marked the beginning of the Civil War.

A Nation Divided

In the following four years, the United States would experience firsthand the consequences of its divisions. The War was not limited to battles between armies; it encompassed clashes of ideologies, economies, and identities. It would be fought across stretches of countryside in legislative chambers on open waters and within people's hearts.

As we conclude this chapter in "The Quick History", let us take a moment to pause and contemplate. The Antebellum period was a tumultuous era in American history characterized by significant changes and paradoxes. It was an era where injustices overshadowed lofty national ideals. These contradictions were the ones that would eventually bring the nation to its challenging moment, putting to the test whether a country founded on freedom and committed to the idea that all individuals are equal could survive for a long time.

8

Civil War and the Reconstruction Period (1861–1877)

The Civil War: Battles, Home Front, and Emancipation 1861–1865

The start of the Civil War

In April 1861, when cannon fire echoed through Fort Sumter in South Carolina, it marked the beginning of armed conflict between the Confederacy and the Union. It marked the end of compromise. Shattered a fragile Union that disagreements for many years had strained. In its youthful stage as a nation, the United States was now facing a test of maturity drenched in blood and characterized by division. This was no quarrel—it had escalated into a full-blown battle for the nation's core values.

Illustrative Portrait of belligerent forces during the Civil War

Let's visualize the nation as a body, a situation where the different parts of the body have arguments about which direction to move, leading to a conflict that causes immense pain and confusion. That's what happened in America in 1861.

Clashes of Ideologies and the Evolving War

The initial battles of the Civil War were a wake-up call for both sides involved. The first significant clash, known as the First Battle of Bull Run (or First Battle of Manassas for the Confederates), occurred on July 21, 1861, near Manassas, Virginia. People from Washington, D.C., came prepared with picnic baskets, expecting a victory by the Union and an entertaining spectacle. Nonetheless, they witnessed a retreat as untrained Union soldiers panicked and fled back to Washington. This event made everyone realize this war would not be swift or glorious.

During these conflicts, people on the home front started feeling the impact of war in their daily lives. Everyday routines were disrupted as resources were redirected to support efforts. Fathers, sons, brothers, and husbands were absent as they enlisted in their armies. Women stepped up into roles traditionally held by men. Took on tasks like managing farms, working in factories, and even serving as battlefield nurses – something almost unheard of before this time. However, the Civil War was more than a struggle for land or power; it represented a fight for the fundamental values of America. The issue of slavery played a role in an unresolved problem that had been ignored for far too long. President Abraham Lincoln, a leader who skillfully navigated through the nation's challenges, initially aimed to preserve the country's unity. Yet, as the war progressed, he understood that achieving freedom was crucial.

This realization led to the Emancipation Proclamation on September 22, 1862. It proclaimed that enslaved people in Confederate-controlled regions would be granted freedom. It's important to note that this Proclamation didn't immediately free all enslaved people since it only applied to Confederate territories and not to slave-holding states within the Union. Nevertheless, it transformed the nature of the conflict by turning it into a fight for liberation.

Lincoln's decision had both strategic considerations. The Proclamation also permitted African-American men to enlist in the Union Army and Navy. This move provided workforce resources for the Union forces.

The American Civil War, a conflict that tore through the nation, persisted beyond its early clashes, intensifying with each passing moment. It seemed as if the entire country became a canvas on which fierce encounters between the blue and gray forces painted brutal scenes of destruction. Among these battles, the significance of the Battle of Antietam stands out due to its immense scale and the opportunities it offered. Opportunities both seized and missed.

On September 17, 1862, Antietam became a chapter in American history as it witnessed the highest number of casualties in a single day; nearly 23,000 lives were lost or forever changed. Imagine a vast field strewn with bodies so densely packed that one could traverse it without touching the ground. The air hangs heavy with the odor of gunpowder mingling with the anguished cries of those wounded and dying. This was where one of the significant battles of the Civil War took place on Union soil. Although it ended in a stalemate, its significance cannot be understated. It bolstered President Lincoln's confidence to issue the definitive Emancipation Proclamation eventually.

Societal Transformations and the War's Aftermath

Let us momentarily shift our focus. What about those who were not bearing rifles or bayonets? What was life like for those left behind their days consumed by labor, anxiety, and anticipation?

For women, this war brought forth unprecedented responsibilities. With a portion of their male counterparts serving in the military, women stepped up to manage farms, plantations, and businesses; they challenged traditional gender roles. They encountered shortages of all varieties—food, medicine, clothing. And had to be resourceful. They resorted to using cloth when cotton became scarce and transformed balconies into makeshift greenhouses for cultivating medicinal herbs.

In the North, while conditions may not have been as dire as in the South, life was still significantly affected by the impact of the war. Women were called upon to contribute their labor in factories, producing ammunition, uniforms, and various supplies to support the war effort. More individuals took on the role of nurses inspired by the groundbreaking efforts of women like Clara Barton, who would later establish the American Red Cross. The war blurred boundaries for women, opening up new opportunities even amidst tragic circumstances.

For African Americans, the war represented a glimmer of hope, a guiding light at the end of an arduous dark tunnel. On January 1, 1863, President Lincoln issued the Emancipation Proclamation, which declared that "all persons held as slaves" within states "are and henceforward shall be free". Although it did not immediately abolish slavery (that would come with the 13th Amendment in 1865), it offered a promise of freedom. Inspired countless Black men to enlist in the Union Army. Their fight extended beyond preserving the Union; it was also about securing their future.

It is crucial to remember that victories in wars are not solely achieved on battlefields but within people's hearts and minds. They stem from sacrifices and the courage to envision a world different from today's. The American Civil War, more than any conflict in the nation's history, represented a clash of ideologies and competing visions for the country's future.

Moving from 1863 to 1864, the war was far from over. President Lincoln appointed General Ulysses S. Grant as commander of all Union armies, which would profoundly impact the course of the conflict. Grant, known for his steadfastness than showmanship, believed in launching aggressive and simultaneous attacks on multiple fronts to deprive the Confederacy of any respite.

With his stern face etched with signs of war weariness, General Grant led his troops through what became known as the Overland Campaign. A series of intense battles fought across Virginia. Capture the explosions, the earth shaking beneath the charge of thousands, and the air itself filled with the cries of fallen soldiers. Amid all this chaos, two intense battles were fought: The Battle of the Wilderness and the Siege of Petersburg. The casualties from these conflicts were so high that they were almost incomprehensible.

Robert E. Lee, leading the Confederacy with brilliance, proved to be a formidable opponent. His soldiers fought unwavering determination to protect their homes and way of life. Despite this, the Union had resources and a workforce coupled with Grant's relentless pressure, which eventually started taking its toll.

In April 1865, we witnessed the acts of this war. Richmond, which served as the Confederate capital, fell into Union hands. After that pivotal moment on April 9, Lee surrendered to Grant at Appomattox Court House. Picture it: two exhausted men from different worlds putting their signatures on a document that ended America's bloodiest conflict.

What did victory indeed mean?

For four million African Americans, it meant liberation—although freedom was accompanied by its challenges. The 13th Amendment was officially ratified in December 1865 and ended slavery in theory. Moreover, the post-war South was a land filled with uncertainty. There was a mix of excitement and uncertainty on the faces of those who tasted freedom for the first time, stepping into a world that was struggling to redefine itself.

The war profoundly disrupted societal roles for women in the North and South. They had experienced independence, shouldered responsibilities, and proved their indispensability. These experiences would lay the groundwork for movements, including the enduring fight for women's suffrage.

As for the nation itself? The United States emerged from the Civil War entirely transformed. The debates over states' rights versus power were settled in favor of a stronger central government. The economy in the North would experience a re-markable surge fueled by rapid industrial expansion. However, this transformation came at a cost; over 600,000 lives were lost, countless others forever changed, and an everlasting shift in our cultural landscape.

Despite these significant changes, America's story was far from complete. Reconstruction loomed ahead as a promise to rebuild our nation, as anyone who has tried to mend something broken knows well enough. Sometimes, even skilled artisans struggle to hide every crack.

Reconstruction and Its Consequences 1865–1877

Reconstruction, political struggles, and racial tensions

As soon as the surrender papers were signed at Appomattox Courthouse, the United States was on the brink of a new era: Reconstruction. Like a ship that had weathered the storm, the nation now faced the immense challenge of repairing its structure, charting its course, and determining what would happen to millions who were no longer treated as property but as citizens.

Illustrated Aftermath of Civil War: Ruins, Hope through Education and Union Troops Depart

The year 1865 marked not only the end of the war but also the beginning of a complex and controversial period that would shape the future of our Union and redefine what American freedom truly meant. President Andrew Johnson, who took over after Lincoln's assassination, had his ideas for Reconstruction often referred to as Presidential Reconstruction.

Consider Johnson, a Southerner with Unionist beliefs. He thought he could navigate the difficult situation by adopting policies towards the South and offering pardons to most former Confederates. But, he severely underestimated the challenges and obstacles he would face.

The Radical Republicans in Congress had distinct intentions. They were appalled when they witnessed how quickly the South implemented laws known as "Black Codes", which were designed to restrict the activities of freed individuals and ensure their availability as a source of cheap labor. Concurrently, a group known as the 'Redeemers' started gaining prominence. Comprising of influential Southern whites, they aimed to reverse the transformative policies of Reconstruction, emphasizing states' rights and white supremacy. The irony is striking – a population that had just tasted freedom found their hopes dashed as they realized liberty as promised came with restrictions, was overshadowed by prejudice, and faced stiff opposition from these 'Redeemers'.

In 1866, things began to change. Congress passed the Civil Rights Act, which affirmed that all individuals born in the United States, regardless of race, were citizens. This challenged the infamous Dred Scott decision of 1857, which stated that African Americans could not be citizens. This act sent shockwaves through centers of power! It was followed by the Fourteenth Amendment in 1868, which aimed to redefine what it truly meant to be an American.

But let's bring it down to reality – what did this mean for ordinary people living in towns and plantations? Imagine a scene where the Freedmen Bureau, established in 1865, worked tirelessly to help enslaved people transition from bondage to lives of freedom. They provided support such as food, housing, and oversight of labor agreements. They even went as far as establishing schools. Picture black women of all ages eagerly holding slates and chalk their hunger for knowledge, evident after years of being denied access to education.

Despite these efforts to progress, resistance was pushing back. The emergence of the Ku Klux Klan and other white supremacist groups resulted in violence and intimidation targeting black Americans and their white allies. Envision the terrifying night riders, the burning crosses symbolizing hate, and the fear they instilled in communities that dared to believe in equality.

The stage was set for a clash between visions and ideals. The Reconstruction era went beyond being a political undertaking; it represented a cultural shift, social transformation, and economic recalibration for a nation that had experienced deep divisions unlike ever before. It became America's test, by fire, to determine if a nation "born out of freedom" could endure while upholding the principle that all individuals are created equal.

Rebuilding the Nation

In 1867, the Reconstruction Acts brought about a shift by imposing military rule over Southern states until their readmission into the Union. It's remarkable to think about Union soldiers patrolling the streets that once echoed with memories of Confederate marches ensuring compliance with laws against the Southern way of life.

Moreover, this period saw African American men gaining voting rights, resulting in the election of politicians at local, state, and even national levels. Hiram Rhodes Revels took his oath as the African American U.S. Senator in 1870—the same year the 15th Amendment was ratified to solidify black men's right to vote.

It was a time filled with contradictions; Mississippi, once the heart of the Confederacy, saw fit to send a black man to represent them in government despite their previous vehement opposition.

However, beneath this surface of progress, there were deep-rooted issues. In 1868, President Johnson faced impeachment, which served as a testament to the political turmoil that engulfed the nation. Despite narrowly surviving the vote for removal from office, this incident highlighted how divided American politics had become.

It is essential not to forget about the citizens whose lives were intertwined with the fabric of history. The families worked together to establish their communities and build schools, churches, and businesses. These individuals shaped their destinies—a phenomenon beautifully captured by establishing historically black colleges and universities like Howard University in 1867.

At the time, many white Southerners—especially those who held power before the war—felt disappointed with what they perceived as Northern domination. They used terms like "carpetbaggers" to describe Northerners who moved South, often using connotations that implied opportunism and exploitation. Additionally, there were those known as "scalawags", whites who supported Reconstruction but were often seen as traitors in their region.

The economy was also changing during this period—a state of flux. While the era of the plantation system, which relied on slavery, had ended, it gave rise to new labor systems such as sharecropping. The cotton fields, once worked by enslaved individuals under harsh conditions, were now managed by men and women who were technically free but trapped in a vicious cycle of debt and dependence that was almost as oppressive.

Amidst these changes, there were the 'Redeemers,' leaders from the South who aimed to reverse the transformations brought about by Reconstruction and "redeem" the region for the population. Their actions eventually led to the Compromise of 1877, an agreement that effectively marked the end of Reconstruction by settling a disputed presidential election. It felt like a long and demanding play reaching its climactic final act with tired actors and an audience uncertain how it would all conclude.

Nevertheless, it's important to note that the story of Reconstruction is not about politics and societal shifts. It is a human tale filled with personal tragedies, triumphs, hopes, and disappointments. It narrates how a nation grappled with finding its way after enduring a dark period with no clear path ahead.

Reconstruction impact

As the 1870s progressed, a sense of fatigue encompassed all aspects. Economic and social. Both in the North and South, the American people grew weary of what they considered the 'Great Experiment' of Reconstruction. This weariness went beyond physical exhaustion; it was a profound weariness seeping into their souls. It was a weariness from a nation's struggle against its historical shackles for over ten years.

In comes 1877. It was a turning point not because of any loud or tumultuous events but due to a quiet agreement that would whisper its way through history. The Compromise of 1877, although perhaps sugarcoating what essentially amounted to a deal, brought resolution to the highly contentious 1876 Presidential election between Rutherford B. Hayes and Samuel J. Tilden. Picture a nation holding its breath with anticipation thick in the air and fear lingering over another civil war.

Then, agreements were made in a room filled with the haze of cigar smoke and palpable tension. As part of the deal for the Presidency, representatives of Hayes consented to withdraw troops from the South, signifying Reconstruction's end. Can you picture the departure of Union soldiers as they left behind a region where the old social order would gradually resurface, akin to ivy reclaiming a long-forgotten ruin? It's crucial to pause and contemplate a question that history often poses: What if? What if there had been no compromise in 1877? What if Reconstruction had continued for another decade? The untaken paths are just as integral to America's narrative as the decisions etched into history books.

Reconstruction's conclusion came from the era of the 'Redeemers' in the South—a period characterized by regaining social control. This renewed order where 'Jim Crow' laws sprouted like unwanted weeds, stifling any progress that had been sown just years earlier. These laws firmly entrenched segregation and stripped African Americans of their rights as a stark reminder that contentious issues surrounding race and equality remained unresolved.

Nevertheless, amidst all this, there were glimmers of hope and progress. The indomitable spirit of humanity shone brightly despite the encroaching darkness. African-American communities did not just survive; they thrived against all odds, establishing institutions and weaving a vibrant cultural tapestry that no laws could diminish. At the time, the American West was alive with its unique challenges and stories serving as a reminder that America was shaped by multiple narratives unfolding simultaneously rather than a single storyline.

When we reflect on the Reconstruction period, it is crucial to view it not as a failed experiment but as a testament to what was possible. It represented a vision of what America could become, even if it took another century to materialize fully.

The characters in our story did not possess the ability to predict the future we now inhabit. However, they had something potent: unwavering faith in the ideals of liberty, equality, and humanity. Thus, the stage was set for the chapter in America's grand historical saga – with new hurdles to overcome, fresh aspirations to pursue, and an unwavering hope driving a nation eternally towards its quest for a "more perfect Union".

Reconstruction Era and Controversial Topics During Reconstruction

Natural environment

As we journey through history during the Civil War and Reconstruction, an often overlooked protagonist played a crucial role, hidden behind the actions of men and military campaigns: nature itself. Immerse yourself in the untouched landscapes of 19th-century America, which stood as a distinct character, providing a backdrop against which history unfurled.

Painting of a cotton field with sharecroppers at work. With a family of African Americans tending to the land

The battles of the Civil War unfolded not only in towns and on battlefields but also across fields, rivers, and forests across America. Consider the significance of the Mississippi River—an intricate serpent carving its way through the core of our nation. This river's control was important strategically and a vital lifeline for the Confederacy. When the Union captured it, it was not only a significant military triumph but also a suffocating effect on the Southern economy. The region heavily relied on the river for transporting goods, especially cotton, which was considered the prized possession of the South.

Furthermore, nature presented its challenges in this situation. While the North had an advantage with its might and the extensive railway network – crucial lifelines during wartime – they also had to contend with natural resistance. Diseases became adversaries that claimed lives more than bullets and bayonets ever could. Dysentery, typhoid fever, and pneumonia showed no mercy towards soldiers, regardless of their uniforms. Even though minié balls (a type of bullet) became synonymous with death during the Civil War, they took far fewer lives than rampant illnesses that swept through closely packed army camps.

As the war persisted, another environmental factor came into play: seasons. General Sherman's "March to the Sea" in the autumn of 1864 turned out to be as much of a battle against nature as it was against Confederate forces. The soldiers faced challenging terrain and rivers to cross, with winter approaching swiftly. Nature proved to be an adversary not easily defeated; its fury affected everyone involved in this conflict regardless of their causes.

As we transitioned into the Reconstruction period, the post-war South experienced changes influenced by its environment. The plantations, the economy's foundation, are now in disarray. The land, exhausted and depleted of nutrients due to practices like monocropping, struggled to produce abundantly as it once did. This environmental toll, combined with the freedom of formerly enslaved people, triggered a notable shift in agricultural practices that would shape the Southern economy and social structure for many generations.

It wasn't the physical landscape that transformed—the period following the Civil War witnessed technological advancements. The expansion of railways, industrial growth, and innovations like telegraphs facilitated more efficient movement of information and goods. Nevertheless, this progress came with its set of challenges for our environment. Deforestation, increased pollution, and urbanization. Consequences that still impact us today.

Now, let's take a moment to reflect on bison—those symbols of the American West. Once upon a time, vast herds roamed freely across the plains; they played a role in ecosystem balance and Plains Indian's livelihoods. However, as the 19th century drew to a close, these magnificent creatures faced a threat of extinction due to relentless hunting. This tragic loss had severe ecological repercussions and profoundly impacted the Native American way of life, intricately intertwined with the bison's existence.

Challenges during Reconstruction

As we uncover layers of history, it becomes evident that Reconstruction was not solely focused on rebuilding shattered lives and infrastructure. It also aimed to heal an environment that actions had wounded. The southern landscape bore scars from deforestation driven by various needs and soil depletion caused by extensive cotton and tobacco cultivation. During this time, people realized that nature carried its scars alongside those borne by its inhabitants.

Moreover, controversies surrounding land ownership and management arose during this period, becoming battles for their right. The policy "40 acres and a mule" symbolized hope for freedmen, representing their aspirations for independence, economic stability, and a positive relationship with the land they had labored on. Unfortunately, President Andrew Johnson's decision to return the confiscated lands to white landowners shattered this hope. Consequently, African Americans had no choice but to engage in a sharecropping system that often resulted in debt and dependence. This controversial choice not only influenced the social structure of the South but also impacted how the land was treated due to the continuous planting of cash crops that depleted soil fertility.

Environmental conservation was not yet widely discussed; nonetheless, signs of its importance emerged. The near extinction of bison herds and extensive deforestation were warnings that unfortunately did not receive sufficient attention amidst the more immediate political and social challenges. Nevertheless, these events played a role in introducing conservationist ideas into American consciousness, which would later flourish in subsequent decades.

This era also witnessed Western expansion fueled by the Homestead Act of 1862. The act offered settlers free access to land, attracting thousands who sought opportunities for resources and advancement. Yet, this policy also faced controversy.

The arrival of settlers in the west disrupted the equilibrium that Native Americans had maintained for centuries. Local ecosystems were disturbed by hunting, habitat destruction, and the introduction of non-native species. Additionally, neglecting indigenous land management practices resulted in soil erosion.

The railroad symbolized progress and unity and brought about environmental changes. Across the country, iron veins stretched out, ushering in urbanization and industry but not without consequences. Picture the landscapes forever transformed by tracks, tunnels, and towns. To acquire land for their expansion plans, railroad companies often resorted to methods that sparked conflicts known as the "Railroad Wars". These tensions primarily revolved around land ownership and corporate greed. It also left lasting environmental impacts as the natural scenery succumbed to this relentless march of "progress".

As we contemplate these controversies, we realize that they were not about land, resources, or technology; they were about power. Who possessed it, who didn't, and how it was exerted. It's tempting to view events as separate incidents, like chapters in a textbook. In the fabric of America, every thread is interconnected. Each event builds upon the last. It paves the way for what follows. The environmental aspects of the Reconstruction era were no exception; they established a narrative that continued long after that period.

Let's think about the impact of deforestation during and after the war. Forests were extensively cleared for farming, shipbuilding, and fueling needs. When the guns fell silent, the sound of axes persisted. The Industrial Revolution in America was voracious, constantly hungry for resources, and never satisfied. The nation's forests once considered resources, were devoured eagerly. This trend persisted until the emergence of the conservation movement in the 19th century when people realized that America's natural resources were not infinite and needed protection and management.

Now, let's consider the plight of the individuals freed from slavery but found themselves trapped by servitude. Share-cropping and tenant farming became prevalent in the South, perpetuating inequality and promoting agricultural practices. For these individuals, the land they cultivated symbolized their freedom and limitations. Unfortunately, Native Americans also continued to face difficulties. The government, influenced by the idea of Manifest Destiny, pushed them away from their lands, resulting in cultural erosion and significant ecological consequences. The buffalo, crucial to tribes' way of life and a vital part of the Great Plains ecosystem, neared extinction due to indiscriminate hunting. In many cases, this hunting was sanctioned or encouraged to control Native populations by depriving them of sustenance.

Amidst all these challenges, America's landscape underwent profound transformations. The expansion of railroads and the discovery of mineral deposits fueled rapid industrialization and urbanization, fundamentally altering the country's physical geography and cultural identity.

Once essential for ecosystems and human communities, rivers

were redirected or contaminated, serving as channels for waste from growing industries. However, amidst this tale of exploitation and hardship, there were glimpses of optimism and resilience. This era witnessed the emergence of movements that advocated for a different connection with nature. Writers and thinkers such as Henry David Thoreau and John Muir began promoting ideas that acknowledged the value of the natural world and the significance of its preservation for future generations. Initially overshadowed by the clamor for progress, these voices gradually gained strength and numbers, ultimately leading to the establishment of the initial national parks and sparking the birth of the American conservation movement. Looking back, it becomes clear that the Civil War and Reconstruction era transcended questions of freedom and governance; they compelled us to reflect on our relationship with the land beneath our feet and the sky above our heads. They challenged us to ponder who we are within the context of nature and what kind of legacy we aspire to leave behind for future generations.

As we bring this chapter to a close and contemplate the Civil War and Reconstruction, we perceive it not only as a time of strife and transformation but also as a pivotal moment in America's ongoing interaction with the natural world. It serves as a reminder that our history encompasses more than the conflicts we engage in with one another; it includes the battles we wage against the environment—and inevitably against ourselves.

V

INDUSTRIALIZATION, WORLD WARS, AND SOCIAL CHANGE

9

From the Gilded Age to WWI: America Transformed (1878–1918)

Industrialization, Labor Movements, Immigration, and Environmental Changes 1878–1913

Labor movements, large-scale immigration

The term "Gilded Age", coined by Mark Twain and Charles Dudley Warner in their 1873 novel, perfectly captures the essence of this period. On the surface, it appeared glamorous and prosperous with wealth. Yet, a closer look revealed rooted issues like poverty, inequality, and exploitation lurking beneath this facade.

Illustration of a 19th-century American landscape, showing the environmental impacts of the Gilded Age

Imagine America at the beginning of this era. The Civil War had ended, and Its repercussions still echoed throughout a nation striving to heal its wounds and unite again. It was a time of transformation for the nation, where everything was on the brink of change. It set the stage for a dance between machines and people as they moved to the rhythm of progress and hardship, hope and despair, dreams and dust.

Then came the railroad—a massive marvel of steel and steam that connected coasts, collapsing distance and time. The awe of those who witnessed a locomotive for the first time was probably unique—the fiery breath of an enormous iron horse—an unmistakable symbol of what was to come! But the railroad meant more than mechanical brilliance; it became the foundation for America's industrial rise. It transported people and goods to faraway markets, bridging the gap between remote towns and bustling cities. However, its impact also sparked economic and social changes that were both revolutionary and disruptive.

Yet amidst this drama, other inventors and innovations in the late 19th century are now taken for granted in today's world. Innovations abounded: Thomas Edison's incandescent light bulb transformed nightscapes, while Alexander Graham Bell's telephone transcended the limitations of physical distance. While Henry Ford is often credited with the assembly line's popularization, it's important to note that the concept pre-dates his innovations. Still, Ford's adaptation significantly transformed production methods.

These changes were more than simple alterations; they were transformations that affected how people perceived things and even the reality itself. Nonetheless, where there is brightness, there are also shadows. The rapid industrialization of this period wasn't limited to the construction of cities; it gave birth to jungles instead. Factories emitted smoke and soot, coloring the sky in shades of gray and black. Workers, including women and children, labored for hours in hazardous and demeaning conditions. Cities expanded rapidly, struggling under the weight of arrivals abroad and in rural America. The tenement houses they lived in were—overcrowded, a far cry from the luxurious mansions occupied by industrial tycoons.

Speaking of these tycoons, it is impossible to discuss this era without mentioning the figures known as the Titans of Industry or, as their critics labeled them, the "Robber Barons". Names like Vanderbilt, Carnegie, Rockefeller, and Morgan became synonymous with wealth and influence. They built railroads, steel production, oil refining, and finance empires. Their opulent mansions, extravagant yachts, and legendary parties captivated people's imaginations. Even though great their wealth was, it came at a cost. One was often borne by laborers who faced wages and grueling working conditions that demanded relentless hours.

The stark difference between the wealthy and the impoverished, the powerful and the powerless, created a backdrop during the Gilded Age: the emergence of the labor movement. Work was no longer an exchange between farmers or artisans and their respective fields or crafts. It transformed into a relationship often exploitative between employers and employees, capital and labor. The harsh working conditions prompted the formation of labor unions and organized strikes and protests— a plea for dignity, respect, and fair remuneration.

As we transitioned from the 19th to the 20th century, these movements gained more cohesion and spread across more expansive areas. The names of unions and their leaders are forever engraved in American history: Knights of Labor, American Federation of Labor (AFL) Samuel Gompers, Mother Jones, and Eugene V. Debs, among others. They fought not through words but sometimes resorting to stones, sticks, and sheer strength in pursuing an eight-hour workday, safer environments, and recognition as individuals rather than mere cogs within an industrialized system.

Now, let's ponder: what defines an American beyond mere birthright or documentation? This question became crucial as America grappled with an influx of immigrants. People from Italy, Ireland, Germany, Poland, China, and various other places arrived with suitcases brimming with dreams. They faced discrimination, hardships, and heartbreaks. Also brought their cultures, cuisines, and aspirations. They had an impact on America while being influenced by it in return.

However, this tale of progress and the clamor of construction wasn't without consequences for the land. Forests were cleared to fuel furnaces, and mountains were depleted for their minerals. Rivers that had flowed for centuries were— diverted while factory smoke polluted the air. The bison, emblematic of untamed wilderness, were pushed to extinction. The environmental toll of industrialization was high and only gradually being comprehended.

Now, at a turning point in history, America stands at a cross-roads. Behind lie fields and farms, while ahead loom cities and smokestacks. The nation stretches its limbs as it reaches for a destiny both awe-inspiring. The scene was set with everyone in their positions. The moment was approaching to begin a period of turmoil and transformation that would shape the next hundred years.

Events and influential individuals who impacted labor movements

The American narrative written with determination, innovation, and diverse perspectives was about to face one of its critical challenges as the 20th century arrived. The Gilded Age wasn't just a stage filled with magnates and struggling workers; it served as a crucible for the modern American identity.

In 1892, an unforgettable labor dispute unfolded: the Homestead Strike. It stands as one of the defining moments in history. An industrial complex called the Homestead Steel Works near Pittsburgh, Pennsylvania, belonged to Andrew Carnegie and was overseen by the relentless Henry Clay Frick. Within its walls, clashes between management and the powerful Amalgamated Association of Iron and Steel Workers erupted due to wage cuts. The conflict escalated dramatically, resulting in a battle between striking workers and Pinkerton agents. Private security is employed to safeguard the plant. Once the dust settled, what remained was a testament to the vast divide between capital and labor. Although the strike was eventually suppressed, with the union being dismantled, it sent a message fighting for workers' rights would be an arduous journey filled with conflicts.

Now, let's turn our attention from industrial furnaces to masses of people arriving on American shores. If factories symbolized this emerging America, immigrants were its lifeblood. They sought refuge in droves to escape poverty, persecution, and hopelessness in their homelands. Ellis Island became synonymous with America's promise when it opened its doors in 1892—an emblem of hope and opportunity for individuals. Contrary to tales of "rags to riches", many immigrants' experience was often of sheer survival.

Think of a boy named Vito from Italy who stepped onto New York City's bustling streets. The cacophony of languages, the towering buildings that create an alien landscape, and the blend of enticing aromas would overwhelm his senses. Like other immigrants, Vito and his fellow newcomers would seek solace in ethnic neighborhoods such as Little Italy, Ireland, or Chinatown. These enclaves offered a reminder of their homelands through familiar languages, food, and customs. Unfortunately, they also faced prejudice during that period. They are portrayed in cartoons as exaggerated caricatures and unfairly blamed for society's problems. Nevertheless, they. Managed to establish themselves in their new homeland by adding their unique contributions to the rich blend of American culture.

In this whirlwind of change, women also began asserting their rights and roles within society. The shirtwaist blouse symbolized the emerging "working woman" and was pivotal in labor reform following the tragic Triangle Shirtwaist Factory fire in 1911. This devastating incident is one of the American industrial disasters claiming the lives of 146 garment workers. Predominantly, young immigrant women perished due to fire-related injuries or smoke inhalation, while some tragically fell or jumped to escape their impending demise. This event impacted the country and led to significant changes in labor laws within the industrial sector. It became a rallying cry for the International Ladies Garment Workers Union (ILGWU) and women's labor movements.

At the time, a relentless pursuit of timber, minerals, and land for agriculture and urbanization caused considerable damage to the American landscape. The majestic forests in the West were cut down plains. Mountains were mined, leaving visible scars across the land. Influential conservationists like John Muir urged the nation to protect its beauty and resources. This led to the establishing of national parks and sparked a widespread discussion on conservation. However, there remained a tension between exploitation and preservation progress and conservation, which would continue as a contentious issue throughout America's journey into the new century.

Despite all its advancements during this era, stark contrasts became evident: wealth alongside poverty, opportunities alongside exploitation, and dreams intertwined with despair. Amidst these dichotomies emerged a resilient spirit of America taking shape – in factories on streets, within people's hearts – uniting newcomers and long-established citizens to forge an identity that would carry them through turbulent years ahead.

We are prompted to reflect on what enduring legacies were left imprinted on history by this period. Beyond the facades of opulent Beaux Arts mansions and beneath the polluted skies, the Gilded Age marked a time of profound change—a reimagining of the "American Dream".

The Pullman Strike & Societal Shifts

Let us examine an event during this era: The Pullman Strike in 1894, a nationwide railway strike originating in Pullman, Illinois. The crux of this conflict lay in the company town concept—where employers owned factories and workers' homes, stores, and often their entire livelihoods. George Pullman, inventor of the Pullman sleeping car, believed he was providing for his workers through his model town. Nevertheless, this idyllic facade shattered rents when wages were reduced without a decrease.

Led by Eugene V. Debs, the strike witnessed a quarter of a million workers across 27 states laying down their tools, disrupting railroad traffic. The government responded swiftly and decisively, using federal troops with the justification that the strike was disrupting mail delivery. The Sherman Antitrust Act was later invoked against labor unions, equating them to illegal combinations or conspiracies in restraint of trade. The overwhelming impact of the strike prompted debates regarding workers' rights versus the influence of monopolies and the role of government in labor disputes.

The cultural diversity brought about by immigrants enriched America's melting pot and introduced tensions. The Chinese Exclusion Act of 1882, which remained in effect until 1943, was a legislative response to economic concerns, particularly on the West Coast. Native-born Americans attributed wage levels to Chinese worker's willingness to work for lower pay. This act set a precedent for immigration restrictions and created divisions—starkly contrasting the Statue of Liberty's iconic call; "Give me your tired, your poor, Your huddled masses yearning to breathe free..."

Amid these challenges, there were moments of triumph. Booker T. Washington, a known African-American educator, writer, and advisor to several presidents, gained national recognition following his speech called the Atlanta Compromise in 1895. Washington emphasized the importance of economic progress to achieve racial equality and upliftment. This belief is beautifully captured in his autobiography titled "Up from Slavery". Additionally, some contemporaries like W.E.B. Du Bois criticized Washington's approach, shedding light on the strategies embraced within the African-American community to attain equality and economic independence.

Similarly, the suffragette movement made strides during this time. Women such as Susan B. Anthony and Elizabeth Cady Stanton became household names as they tirelessly fought for women's right to vote. The formation of the National American Woman Suffrage Association in 1890 played a critical role in this struggle and laid the foundation for the eventual ratification of the 19th Amendment in 1920.

Furthermore, one cannot overlook the technological advancements of that era. Guess people's awe when they experienced moving walkways and towering Ferris wheels and even tasted a tantalizing invention called "chewing gum" at the 1893 World Columbian Exposition in Chicago! It was a time of marvels—a testament to ingenuity that offered a glimpse into what lay ahead in the wondrous 20th century.

When we reflect on the Gilded Age, it becomes clear that it

encompassed more than another chapter in American history. It was a story of struggle, negotiation aspirations, and disappointment, creating an identity that would soon face challenges on a global scale as America was called to enter a new era marked by war.

World War I 1914- 1918

Picture this: a world rapidly shrinking before our eyes. The 20th century began with nations becoming more interconnected through steamships, telegraphs, and conflicting ideologies of unity or division. The Great War, later known as World War I, was against this backdrop. Erupted like a storm across the globe. Initially, America observed this storm from a distance. President Woodrow Wilson was re-elected under the slogan "He kept us out of war" and advocated for neutrality. One might ask, what did "neutrality" mean in a world that seemed to be getting smaller daily? As Europe became engulfed in conflict, America grappled with its identity, whether to remain a sanctuary of peace or emerge as an influential global power. The war began with the assassination of Archduke Franz Ferdinand of Austria-Hungary in June 1914. This event catalyzed a Europe divided by nationalism, imperial ambitions, and complex alliances.

In the beginning, many Americans saw the war as a noise, like an argument happening in another part of the world. However, as the world became smaller and more interconnected, the effects of the war started to reach the United States. Trade disruptions, stories from immigrants from warring countries, and powerful propaganda that depicted both heroism and horrors all contributed to this.

There were specific incidents that significantly changed how Americans felt about the war. For instance, when a German U-boat sank the British ocean liner RMS Lusitania in 1915 and caused 128 deaths, it ignited national outrage. Additionally, when news spread about intercepted communication known as the Zimmermann Telegram—an offer from Germany to Mexico for an alliance if America joined World War I—public opinion in America became even more inflamed. Moreover, Germany's unrestricted submarine warfare directly threatened ships and eroded their commitment to neutrality.

At this point in history—when war drums were growing louder—it is essential to pause and imagine what life was like for Americans. A farmer in the Midwest reading headlines about battles happening far away in trenches or an immigrant factory worker in New York City anxiously worrying about family members caught up in Europe's turmoil. Picture the conversations in households, street corners, and local newspapers, where people debate whether America should involve itself in the fight for democracy abroad or stay committed to preserving its principles of freedom and self-determination at home.

As tensions escalated, President Wilson addressed Congress in April 1917 with a statement; "The world must be made safe for democracy". The United States, comprised of immigrants, ideologists, innovators, and isolationists alike, was thrust into a conflict. This marked a departure from its policy of isolationism and signaled the emergence of America as a new global power.

American involvement went beyond words. The country mobilized over four million military personnel, reshaping civilian life through war industries and propaganda campaigns promoting Liberty Bonds to support the war effort. Women already fighting for their right to vote stepped into roles previously held by men. Additionally, the Great Migration saw a movement of African Americans from rural areas in the South to Northern cities as they sought employment in war-related industries. This demographic shift had lasting effects on the nation's map.

Illustration of 1917 Town Square: Politicians, War Talks, and Uncle Sam's Call

Under the leadership of General John J. Pershing, the American Expeditionary Forces played a role in tipping the scales on the Western Front. Notably, the Battle of the Argonne Forest is a testament to American forces' military strength and sacrifice, resulting in over 26,000 U.S. Soldiers losing their lives in one of the most lethal battles ever fought in American history.

Home front, societal changes, and the global stage

The resounding artillery echoes were not limited to distant shores; they initiated transformations that reverberated through American households and touched hearts. While our soldiers courageously faced grueling trench warfare in Europe, life at home underwent its kind of trench warfare. The entire nation was fully engaged in a state of war. What did "total war" mean for those not holding rifles on the front lines?

Factories that once manufactured consumer goods swiftly transitioned into war industries overnight, producing an abundance of artillery shells, airplanes, and uniforms. This shift was not solely industrial; it had societal implications as well. Traditionally confined to roles, women took on new roles in these factories, even wearing work trousers. Conceive the shift this brought about – propaganda posters featuring predecessors to "Rosie the Riveter" encouraged women to join the workforce and challenge traditional gender norms.

These shifts brought about a cultural transformation foreshadowing the subsequent movements for women's liberation. At the time, the war played a role in expediting the Great Migration. African Americans experiencing the realities of Southern sharecropping and Jim Crow laws began relocating to northern regions in considerable numbers for the first time. Their goal was to secure employment opportunities amidst the economic boom and to escape the oppressive segregation prevalent in the South. This demographic shift laid a foundation for civil rights movements and permanently transformed cities such as Chicago, Detroit, and New York. These growing communities witnessed an upsurge in jazz music, literature, and an emerging sense of social identity that set the stage for what would become known as the Harlem Renaissance.

Regardless, not all changes brought outcomes. Fear often accompanies conflicts, and World War I was no exception. The government enacted the Espionage Act of 1917 and the Sedition Act of 1918 to suppress dissenting voices, resulting in over 2,000 prosecutions. Propaganda aimed not at boosting morale or promoting war bonds but also at fostering distrust towards anyone deemed "un-American." Suspicion among neighbors grew rampant; individuals with German ancestry were partic- ularly scrutinized. Sauerkraut was renamed "liberty cabbage". German measles became "liberty measles". While speaking German could lead to violence or ostracization by society.

Food also became a symbol of patriotism during that time. Herbert Hoover, who would later become president, led the U.S. Food Administration—encouraged Americans to ration their food voluntarily. "Meatless Tuesdays" and "Wheatless Wednesdays" became widely known as part of the effort to support troops overseas.

The entry of the United States into the war had ramifications beyond the Allies' home fronts. American soldiers and resources played a role in a conflict that had previously been stuck in a brutal stalemate. With troops and substantial resources provided by the U.S. and new strategies like the convoy system to counter U-boat attacks, the tide of the war slowly turned.

In 1918, the Allies carried out significant offensives with support from American forces. The Hundred Days Offensive was a series of attacks throughout the summer and fall that ultimately broke through Germany's final line of defense, known as the Hindenburg Line. Yet, these victories did not come without sacrifices. The outbreak of the Spanish Flu pandemic in 1918 affected military camps severely, causing more deaths than even those caused directly by warfare itself. This grim reality underscored how vulnerable our interconnected world had become.

The collective relief was felt worldwide when the armistice was signed on the 11th day of the 11th month in 1918. Soldiers, covered in mud and haunted by the horrors of trench warfare, finally allowed themselves to dream about going. Yet, when they did return, they found that the world had changed drastically. The war supposed to end all wars had planted seeds for conflicts. The harsh terms of the Treaty of Versailles set the stage for discontent, which ultimately led to the rise of fascism in the years that followed.

The United States transformed as a result of World War I. It proved itself as a military, potentially moral superpower on a global scale. At what cost? What did it truly gain? The lessons from this war were numerous, but they were as complicated and diverse as those who learned them.

After WWI

After all, guns fell silent, and people around the globe struggled to comprehend what had just happened. The losses were overwhelming. The landscapes suffered irreversible damage. The aftermath of World War I brought about a shattered world order, creating a void that new ideologies rushed to fill. It wasn't about rebuilding what was lost but also about envisioning a new world and what it could—and should—be.

1919, the Paris Peace Conference convened to outline peace terms after World War I. President Woodrow Wilson arrived in France with his Fourteen Points, which outlined a blueprint for a global order. These points included proposals for trade, transparent agreements, democracy, and, most importantly, creating an international organization called the League of Nations. Its purpose was to ensure "guarantees of political independence and territorial integrity for the both large and small nation".

However, not everyone fully embraced Wilson's vision. Britain and France, still reeling from the war's devastation and mourning their losses, sought retribution from Germany. As a result, the Treaty of Versailles imposed reparations and territorial concessions on the Germans. Of fostering reconciliation as intended, this punitive approach planted seeds of resentment and economic instability—ultimately setting the stage for the outbreak of World War II.

Meanwhile, in the United States, internal struggles were taking place.

The Senate's rejection of the Treaty of Versailles and the League of Nations due to concerns about getting involved in conflicts has led to numerous historical debates. People have questioned whether it was a move to protect American sovereignty or a step back from America's destined global leadership role.

Beyond the end of the war, society continued to face challenges. The transition from war to peace brought about difficulties. The Red Scare of 1919 and 1920 created a fear of Bolshevism and radical leftist ideologies following the Russian Revolution. This fear resulted in raids and deportations during the Palmer Raids. The nation also experienced labor strikes as workers sought to regain rights suspended during wartime while racial tensions escalated and violence increased, including the Tulsa Race Massacre.

Amidst all this turmoil, there was room for innovation and a sense of freedom. The Jazz Age was coming, bringing creativity and joy in response to suffering. Additionally, women achieved a milestone in their fight for rights with the ratification of the 19th Amendment in 1920, granting them the right to vote. These developments didn't completely erase the wounds left by the war. They provided a glimpse into a society capable of immense transformation. And the potential of what America could still become.

During this period, there was a clash between traditionalism versus modernism, isolationism versus internationalism, and fear versus freedom. This cultural earthquake affected every aspect of society. Literature, art, and philosophy reflected a sense of disappointment with the ways and a search for new meaning. Writers of the Lost Generation, like Ernest Hemingway and F. Scott Fitzgerald, explored themes of disillusionment and the search for purpose in a fragmented world. The Harlem Renaissance sparked an explosion of American culture and intellectualism that resonated through art, music, and literature.

World War I was both a conflict and a catalyst for significant change. It is an essential chapter in American history and global history. It is a tragic reminder of the costs of conflict while highlighting the resilience of humanity's spirit. It redefined borders, ideologies, and international global power structures, setting the stage for the events of the 20th century. However, despite being called "The War to End All Wars", it did not achieve its aspiration. Instead, it taught us a lesson about the outcomes of nationalism, imperialism, and militarism. At the time, it paved the way for America to rise as a powerful force on the global stage.

The Role of Technology in Industrialization and War

The 20th-century innovation

While the Gilded Age and Progressive Era had already set the stage, World War I pushed advancements forward due to sheer necessity. This war was unlike any other before it. The romanticized notions of battle, with charges and duels, clashed with the reality of trench warfare, machine guns, and chemical weapons.

Portrait of a 20th-century industrial factory, signifying the rapid industrialization brought about by technolog

It served as a wake-up call, a harsh lesson that warfare had undergone changes and survival now relied on adaptation and innovation. The advancements made during this era weren't solely intended for war purposes. They seeped into life, forever transforming society. Let's focus on the battlegrounds, where the urgent nature of war sparked a technological race.

During World War I, the relatively new invention of the airplane took on a whole new significance. What were once fragile structures made of wood and fabric quickly evolved into combat machines. The skies became a battlefield as reconnaissance aircraft transformed into fighters and bombers. Just imagine the mix of wonder and terror experienced by soldiers witnessing combat for the first time. The once neutral skies now turned into theaters of war.

Tanks also debuted during this period, rumbling across no man's land with machine gun fire that decimated infantry units. They were slow, cumbersome, and often unreliable. Symbolized a new approach to warfare—one dominated by mechanized armor and mobility. Nevertheless, perhaps the unsettling innovation was chemical warfare. Poison gases, like chlorine and mustard gas, introduced a killer that spared no one in its path.

Soldiers searched for gas masks, facing an enemy without regard for borders or distinguishing between targets. This sneaky method of warfare demonstrated an abandonment of any sense of chivalry in conflict, making it clear that the war aimed not only at soldiers but at the very essence of their humanity.

Meanwhile, these years were marked by significant and transformative changes on the home front. Introducing electricity illuminated cities and towns, altering lifestyles and work environments. The telephone, radio, and the early days of the motion picture industry brought people together and provided entertainment during a time when war was raging overseas. Women stepped up to fill the roles left vacant by men who were away at war. They found themselves increasingly involved with technology both in factories and offices. This shift wasn't a temporary adjustment; it began a broader societal transformation regarding gender roles and workforce dynamics.

It's significant to note that technology was more than a tool for progress; it also reflected society's values and fears. The misguided eugenics movement gained popularity during this time as a distorted interpretation of Darwin's theories. It advocated for controlled breeding to "improve" the race. This served as a reminder that not all scientific endeavors are noble and progress itself is not always positive.

As we continue our journey through this period, we will delve deeper into the impact of technological advancements that emerged or were accelerated by the necessities of war. These advancements gradually permeated life, reshaping convenience, entertainment, and human interaction.

Rapid changes

The whirlwind of progress in the early 20th century transformed battlefields, revolutionizing American homes, industries, and even how people worked and enjoyed leisure time. Picture yourself in this era: cities expanding skywards and outwards, streets buzzing with automobiles, invisible radio waves crackling. It was an age where science seemed magical, with each passing day bringing new conveniences and wonders that were once considered mere fantasies.

The typical American home transitioned from relying on candlelight and wood for illumination and warmth to embracing electricity. The introduction of lighting changed how people lived and worked by extending the hours of productivity. The familiar sounds of household appliances like vacuum cleaners, washing machines, and toasters became synonymous with an era of efficiency and modernity. These luxurious items quickly became essential in every progressive household.

At the time, a revolution was taking place in American industry. Although the assembly line had been around since the previous century, it reached its pinnacle in the early 20th century thanks to innovators like Henry Ford. With his advancements, automobiles became accessible to the masses. Picture those factories: a harmonious blend of man and machine working together seamlessly. Each worker played a role like a musical note in a symphony while each machine contributed its precise rhythm. This wasn't manufacturing but a synchronized dance of productivity that propelled the United States to economic prominence.

Yet this technological revolution had its drawbacks as well. While symbolizing efficiency, the assembly line also brought monotony and dehumanization to workers. Upton Sinclair's "The Jungle" exposed the reality of industrialization, where speedy production overshadowed fundamental human rights. This dichotomy between progress driven by innovation and exploitation emerged as a theme during this era.

Communication methods were also changing during this time. The telephone revolutionized communication, allowing voices to travel across cities, states, and the Atlantic Ocean. The radio became a part of homes, bringing families together to listen to news, music, comedies, and dramas. It was an era of burgeoning content and opportunities. During this time, entertainment and information became more accessible than before.

Let's not forget about the cinema – a remarkable technological breakthrough that transformed storytelling. The silent silver screen served as a canvas for conveying emotions through actors' exaggerated expressions depicting tales of love, tragedy, and comedy. Then came "The Jazz Singer", heralding the arrival of "talkies", where suddenly the screen could speak, sing and play music. This innovation deepened the experience for audiences.

These advancements weren't just shaping lifestyles; they were shaping a new cultural landscape. Urbanization gained momentum as people flocked to cities to pursue jobs and the allure of urban life. This shift created a mosaic as diverse populations intertwined – each group adding their unique thread to the tapestry of American identity.

Not to mention, beneath this progress lay inequalities. Not everyone had access to the new technologies. Rural areas were left behind compared to centers, and the poor could hardly afford what the middle class considered normal. Moreover, the workforce that fueled this surge struggled with harsh working conditions, leading to labor movements and growing calls for reform.

As we delve deeper into this era, we will closely examine how these technological advancements, with their glimmers of hope, also cast shadows. They brought forth ethical dilemmas and societal challenges that Americans grappled with amidst rapid change.

Progress

The lightning-fast pace of innovation in the early 20th century brought forth a paradigm shift—a complete redefinition of what it meant to be alive in this bold and unfamiliar world. However, it also prompted contemplation and occasional concern about our human essence. Were we adapting at a rate to keep up with such rapid change? Let's explore the aspect hidden behind the buzzing machines and bustling airwaves. Technology had an impact on women's lives both in major and minor ways. Everyday household appliances may seem ordinary. They lightened the physical load of domestic work even though expectations for domestic perfection increased simultaneously. Women discovered career paths as typists, telephone operators, and department store clerks in the shimmering cityscapes. The typewriter and telephone symbols of modernity became tools for women's liberation by opening doors to the world and providing a certain level of financial independence.

We should also consider the influence of automobiles – vehicles that offer a newfound freedom by breaking down distance barriers. Young people could court each other without supervision, while families could enjoy Sunday drives that provided a sense of independence and leisure previously unimaginable. Nonetheless, there were drawbacks. Streets became places with an increase in accidents and negative impacts on the environment. The love affair with automobiles began to reveal its flaws.

Let us also contemplate the Great Migration, one of the most significant internal movements of people in American history. Millions of African Americans migrated from the South to cities in the North, driven by a longing to escape racial violence and economic struggles. The prospect of jobs lured them, but unfortunately, they encountered new forms of discrimination and hardships in their new urban environments. Nevertheless, these cities became cultural hubs where the Harlem Renaissance flourished, showcasing the remarkable talents of African-American artists, musicians, and writers.

Of note, technological advancements during this time increased factory productivity but also contributed to more devastating warfare. The introduction of weapons, tanks, and machine guns made World War I one of the deadliest conflicts in history. The profound trauma experienced by soldiers on the lines had a lasting impact on an entire generation, which found expression through art and literature produced during that era.

As we wrap up our exploration of this period, it is crucial to acknowledge that every step forward came with ethical dilemmas, moral quandaries, and societal challenges. The stories told by those who lived through these times—their aspirations, struggles, and resilience—serve as a testament to the strength of spirit. Their experiences compel us to reflect upon our relationship with technology and progress—an inquiry that remains as relevant today as it was a century ago.

In the next chapter, we will move away from the chaos of World War and the rapid growth of industries to a period that stands out for its striking differences: the Roaring Twenties, a time characterized by vibrant cultural changes and economic success, which was then followed by the harsh desperation of the Great Depression.

10

Between Wars: Roaring Twenties to WWII (1919–1945)

Social and Cultural Changes in the Interwar Period 1919–1939

The Roaring Twenties: Prelude to the Great Depression

After World War I ended, America was eager to put behind the horrors it had witnessed and return to a sense of normalcy. What did "normal" mean in a world forever changed by war? The Roaring Twenties, or Jazz Age, emerged as America's response. It was a decade filled with contrasts—a mix of prosperity, cultural revolution, and underlying disillusionment. Despite living on the edge of uncertainty, people were ready to dance away their worries.

A portrayal of the era's dichotomy: a jazz club's energy juxtaposed with the Dust Bowl's somber reality

As the 1920s began, soldiers returned from Europe carrying not only memories of war but also new styles, cultures, and ideas they had encountered abroad. The world seemed smaller now. American men were eager to embrace this newfound global influence and celebrate life anew. So, how did they manage to achieve it? They embraced all the defining elements of the decade: jazz music, rebellious flappers, secret speakeasies, and a never-ending celebration.

Let's detour and begin our story in an unlikely setting: a car factory. Henry Ford's assembly line, tirelessly producing Model Ts, wasn't just manufacturing automobiles; it was giving birth to a consumer culture. The introduction of credit and the "buy now pay later" philosophy made the American Dream appear attainable for ordinary individuals. The automobile granted freedom and transformed cities while redefining what it meant to be truly free. It became more than a means of transportation; it symbolized prosperity and significantly shaped individual identities.

Nevertheless, beneath the surface of this era lay hidden currents of discontent. The Red Scare between 1919 and 1920 intensified fears of communism and anarchism, leading to crackdowns on perceived radicals, including immigrants. The infamous case of Sacco and Vanzetti serves as a reminder of the fear and prejudice that permeated society during this time—a nation struggling to come to terms with the rapid cultural and political changes unfolding before them.

Prohibition, commencing in 1920, is another example of the contradictions that defined this decade. In an attempt to control activities, the outcome was quite the opposite, as it gave rise to organized crime and a general disregard for the law. The underground bars, known as speakeasies, were bustling with activity. They fell under the control of notorious gangsters like Al Capone in Chicago. This unintended consequence demonstrated how complex human behavior can be and highlighted the results of seemingly straightforward policies.

The jazz music that echoed throughout that era symbolized a cultural shift. It represented the spirit of the times, blending African rhythms, southern blues, and urban soul. Despite being associated with marginalized communities, jazz transcended boundaries and had people from all over the country tapping their feet. It was a form of expression that defied traditional music norms and reflected those years' fast-paced and improvisational nature.

Women who contributed significantly during wartime were no longer willing to be confined to conventional societal roles. The 19th Amendment, ratified in 1920, marked a stride towards gender equality by granting women the right to vote. Embodying newfound freedom for women was the flapper – her bobbed hair, short skirts, and carefree demeanor represented this liberation. She wasn't simply a fashion statement; she described a declaration of independence from the corsets of the past.

Still, not everyone celebrated this change. Many in rural areas, particularly among conservative Protestant communities, observed these shifts with dismay. The Ku Klux Klan, which experienced a resurgence in the 1920s, found fertile ground to spread its messages of religious and traditional moral purity. The Scopes "Monkey" Trial in 1925 symbolized the clash between science and religion, modernism and traditionalism. Meanwhile, during the 1920s, the Harlem Renaissance was reshaping African-American identity. Influential figures such as Langston Hughes, Zora Neale Hurston, and Louis Armstrong were not just artists; they played roles in revitalizing African-American culture by creating stories of resilience, pride, and remarkable creativity in the face of hardship.

When depicting this era, it is crucial to acknowledge both the positives and negatives—the advancements made and the underlying resistance. The story of the 1920s encompasses more than economic prosperity and cultural liberation; it also includes social tensions stemming from clashes between old traditions and new ideas—a nation navigating its path after experiencing history's first global war.

Yet few realized that as time passed throughout this decade, there would be a shift in rhythm on the horizon. The signs were evident for those who could interpret them: the production, the risky investments, and the unstable foundations of economic success. In 1929, everything came crashing down.

Changes

The 1920s appeared to represent progress and modernity with their glitz and jazz. However, every good story has its turns. Beneath all that prosperity and celebration lay rooted issues. Fractures that would soon plunge our nation into one of its most challenging times: The Great Depression.

As society embraced the Jazz Age enthusiastically, it also embraced an unwavering belief in continuous growth. The stock market became an indicator of American prosperity. Essentially becoming America's pulse. Unfortunately, speculation ran wild due to inadequate government regulations at that time. Ordinary Americans were swept up in a frenzy of get-quick schemes, investing their hard-earned savings into the stock market. A nation captivated by the belief that there were no limits to success.

But not everyone was included in this wave of prosperity. While urban areas thrived, the agricultural sector, a significant part of the American economy, struggled. Farmers who had expanded their production during World War I faced drops in prices and overwhelming debt during the post-war period. These challenges in areas were early indications of an approaching storm but went largely unnoticed amidst the bustling noise of city life.

Furthermore, a troubling reality lies beneath the surface of growth: income inequality. The wealthy reveled in wealth, while average workers saw slight wage improvement. It was as if the country was attending a feast where only a few indulged while many were left with mere crumbs. This imbalance created a society teetering on a balance beam far more precarious than most people realized. Another significant challenge of this era was the issue of race. The Great Migration witnessed numbers of African Americans relocating to northern cities for better opportunities and freedom from the overt racial segregation prevalent in the South. Nevertheless, they soon discovered that even the North faced challenges, and promises were not easily fulfilled.

Segregation remained a reality, resulting in racial tensions and violence due to the fierce competition for jobs and housing. The Harlem Renaissance, a cultural movement, also served as an act of resilience against the prevailing systemic racism and inequality. The story takes a turn on October 29, 1929, infamously known as Black Tuesday. This was when the stock market crashed, wiping billions of dollars of wealth in one day. The bursting of the bubble had consequences. Banks collapsed, and businesses shut down. Millions were left unemployed. Thus began the era of the Great Depression.

How did Americans cope with this sudden and stark depriva-tion? How does a nation accustomed to soaring prosperity deal with such a blow? At first, there was disbelief followed by panic. Even those who had never experienced poverty found themselves struggling to survive. The emergence of shantytowns mockingly referred to as "Hoovervilles," named after President Herbert Hoover, became symbols of despair.

The Great Depression wasn't solely a crisis but profoundly impacted culture and psychology. The cherished ideals of self-reliance and "rugged individualism" that Americans took pride in were questioned. This crisis shook the nation's foundations, challenging its beliefs about freedom, capitalism, and the American Dream. However, in these darkest moments, the resilient spirit of the American people was evident. Families and communities came together to support each other and ensure survival. By relying solely on money, bartering became a common practice for trading skills and goods. Amidst the immense hardships, new art and literature emerged, reflecting the unfiltered realities of the American experience.

As the 1930s began, the United States was on the edge of a precipice. The Great Depression went beyond an economic downturn; it became a nationwide traumatic event that would profoundly reshape the country's political, social, and cultural fabric. While the Roaring Twenties had set a stage, nobody anticipated such a harsh curtain fall.

It's important to remember that history is not merely a series of incidents but an interconnected tapestry. The conclusion of the 1920s brought forth desperation. Also planted seeds for renewal. A radical reevaluation of the government's role in people's lives that would later be known as the New Deal. That narrative will be explored in our upcoming segment.

The Dust Bowl and the inception of the New Deal

When America was shaken to its core by a visitor called the Great Depression, the nation faced an identity crisis as opportunities vanished and prosperity faded. It wasn't about numbers and statistics; it was about real people with dreams, families struggling to survive, and communities grappling with despair.

To make matters worse, there was also a catastrophe known as the Dust Bowl. Envision dust storms casting darkness upon the skies, sometimes even reaching as far as the East Coast. This left a path of devastation across the Great Plains. Failed agricultural practices combined with drought transformed what was once considered "the breadbasket of the world" into a hopeless landscape. Families in these heartland areas, already battered by collapse, now faced destruction at almost apocalyptic levels.

This era was not a chapter in a history book; it represented a struggle for survival against the forces of nature and human mistakes. During these times, Americans sought hope, which they found in Franklin D. Roosevelt (FDR). His victory in the 1932 election marked a significant shift in American politics. FDR's New Deal, consisting of a series of programs and initiatives in two phases, aimed at recovery and reform, offering relief to those in need and promising an economic boost. Picture the nation gathering around their radios, leaning closer to catch every word of FDR Fireside Chats—a series of radio addresses where the president spoke directly to the American people as if he were in their living rooms. These chats were more than informative sessions; they served as an emotional lifeline—a symbol that a leader had taken charge during the nation's most challenging times.

The New Deal was an unprecedented endeavor that completely transformed the country's landscape. From constructing schools and hospitals to establishing Social Security, to undertaking public works projects like the Hoover Dam, and providing support for artists, musicians, and writers through initiatives such as the Works Progress Administration—the New Deal went beyond being mere policy; it sparked a revolution.

It reshaped the way the federal government was perceived by Americans, transforming it from an entity to a direct source of support and care. On the other hand, the New Deal had its flaws. Critics argued that it gave the government power and led to an increase in national debt. Moreover, specific New Deal programs discriminated against African Americans due to local implementation often depriving them of opportunities and benefits. This is a stark reminder that setbacks can sometimes accompany progress.

During the Depression, women made significant contributions, although historical accounts often overlooked these efforts. Eleanor Roosevelt, FDR's wife, was not merely a background figure; she redefined the role of First Lady by advocating for human rights, women's issues, and children's causes. She acted as FDR's representative across the nation, sharing stories of hardship and resilience from its people. Picture her: a woman navigating a male-dominated world while making her voice heard.

As the 1930s ended, another major global event was on the horizon. One that would have reaching consequences. The winds of war were sweeping across Europe and Asia. The wounds of the Great Depression were still fresh in the United States when a global conflict of scale drew the nation's attention. It was a time when economic hardship and conflicting ideologies challenged the foundations of the free world.

In our portrayal of America's story, the Great Depression holds significance. It served as a turning point that shaped the nation's character, exposing its vulnerabilities while also revealing its strength. It demonstrated that America's true power resided not in its wealth but in its people—its resilience and ability to adapt and conquer adversity.

As we conclude this segment, it becomes evident that events do not merely shape history; the indomitable spirit of humanity drives it. This spirit, which endured through despair, would soon face another test: war.

World War II: Frontlines and Home Front 1939–1945

Dynamics of the battlefronts

Whispers of war gradually grew louder by the 1930s. The conflicts brewing in lands appeared to many Americans as distant rumblings—a sense of foreboding yet far away. Though, it became evident that a storm was approaching—an encompassing and profound conflict that would reshape the foundations of the global order.

Portrait illustrating World War II's major milestones

Let's begin by setting the stage. The world in the 1930s was depicted with tension as fascism, communism, and democratic capitalism engaged in ideological battles. The Axis powers— Germany, Italy, and Japan—pursued aggressive expansionist policies that violated international agreements and boundaries. Meanwhile, the Allied powers, including the United Kingdom, France, the Soviet Union, which later joined the Allies during the war, China, and eventually the United States, aimed to counteract the progress of the Axis forces. However, before the attack on Pearl Harbor, America was deeply entrenched in isolationism due to its weariness from World War I and the burdens of the Great Depression.

December 7, 1941, was a turning point in our story. It was when Pearl Harbor came under attack. Picture the chaos that ensued: burning ships, thunderous explosions, and, most importantly, the shock of this assault. It was this event that thrust America onto a position on the global stage as a combatant. President Roosevelt famously declared it "a date which will live in infamy." The nation found itself at war. A conflict that would demand strength and unity from every individual.

World War II wasn't just a series of battles on distant lands; its impact reverberated within American factories, homes, and communities. Consider how American industries transformed; automobile manufacturers shifted gears to produce tanks; typewriter companies diversified into firearm production; and let us not forget about women! They courageously stepped into roles traditionally held by men. Riveters, welders, and electricians became iconic figures known as "Rosie The Riveters." These women symbolized empowerment and patriotism while keeping our nation's gears turning. That being said, we must not forget about the American community, who faced a peculiar situation. They fought for freedom in countries while experiencing inequality and discrimination at home. This dual struggle, known as the "Double V Campaign," aimed to achieve victory against fascism and racism domestically. Despite facing segregation and discrimination within the Armed Forces and on soil, over a million African Americans served with distinction during the war.

Additionally, we cannot overlook the plight of Americans, who endured a dark chapter in U.S. History. Following the attack on Pearl Harbor and out of fear of espionage or sabotage, President Roosevelt signed Executive Order 9066, which led to the internment of 120,000 Japanese Americans—many of whom were American citizens. Families were uprooted from their lives. Sent to hastily constructed camps—a regrettable blemish on our nation's wartime record.

This conflict was more than a clash of weapons; significant technological advancements also marked it. Radar technology, jet engines, medical practices—and perhaps most ominously—nuclear energy all played crucial roles. Scientists and engineers became as essential to the war effort as soldiers. The Manhattan Project operated under secrecy as it raced to harness atomic power—a race that would ultimately create an unimaginably powerful weapon.

Amid World War II, the battle lines stretched across landscapes and continents. Each soldier had a story woven with threads of courage, fear, companionship, and heartbreak. Envision young men, many in their teenage years, hailing from all walks of American life. They trudged through the freezing forests of Ardennes, felt the scorching heat of North African deserts, and waded through the crashing waves of the Pacific Ocean while facing relentless enemy fire.

Now, picture the European skies resonating with the hum of Allied air fleets. During that time, there were the Tuskegee Airmen, who were the African American military aviators. They decided to paint the tails of their planes, which earned them the nickname "Red Tails." Despite facing oppression, they soared high. Shattered false beliefs of racial inferiority with each successful mission.

Among the many pivotal moments of World War II, one stands out: the Normandy landings, commonly called D-Day. With extensive planning and the advantage of deception, the Allies carried out the largest amphibious invasion in history on the beaches of Normandy, France, on June 6, 1944.

Imagine this scene: As dawn broke, a fleet of more than 5,000 vessels extended across the horizon, transporting nearly 160,000 troops. As these courageous men made their way onto beaches codenamed Utah, Omaha, Gold, Juno, and Sword, they encountered German fortifications, machine gun nests, and entrenched positions. The battle's intensity, especially with the high casualty rates at Omaha Beach, made it an incredibly harrowing experience for many.

Nevertheless, the sacrifices made by those who fought and those who lost their lives during D-Day and in the Battle of Normandy laid a solid foundation for liberating Western Europe from Nazi control. The success of these operations marked a turning point that eventually led to Germany's defeat in Europe. By August of that year, Paris had been liberated as Allied forces marched through its streets.

The Normandy invasion showcased individual soldiers' bravery and resilience and highlighted practical cooperation among Allied forces. The accounts that emerged from these shores showcasing unity, sacrifice, and an unwavering spirit symbolized the Allied campaign in Europe. But the battlefields weren't only in far-off lands. The home front was also a battlefield where propaganda, rationing, and civil defense drills were commonplace. Children collected scrap metal families cultivated "Victory Gardens" to supplement rationed goods. Movies, radio broadcasts, and newspapers entertained, informed, and fueled patriotism.

In this war environment, societal norms underwent significant changes. Women took on roles left by men at war and discovered newfound independence and capability. It wasn't about doing men's work but proving that gender has no bearing on one's abilities. However, many women were expected to leave their jobs and return to domestic life when the war ended. This expectation set the stage for battles over gender roles in America.

In parallel, the minority groups aimed to leverage their contributions during wartime for civil rights. During World War II, Mexican Americans faced a set of challenges. Many of them worked in agricultural roles or served in the military. Yet, they faced discrimination while contributing to the war effort. The "Zoot Suit Riots" in 1943 in Los Angeles highlighted these tensions as Mexican-American youths were violently targeted.

Native Americans also played roles during the war, with over 44,000 bravely serving in the military. The Navajo Code Talkers gained recognition for their contribution by creating an unbreakable code based on their native language. This code played a role in several battles fought in the Pacific region. Utilizing their heritage as a hidden weapon, they made honorable contributions to the war effort that honored their ancestors.

As we explore deeper into this period of conflict, we witness a complex collage unfold before us—not victories and defeats on battlefields but also societies undergoing profound changes. The war disrupted established norms. Laid the groundwork for transformation that would take decades to materialize fully.

Nevertheless, amidst tales of courage and societal transformations, we must confront one of the chapters of this war—the Holocaust. American soldiers who liberated Nazi concentration camps bore witness to horrifying evidence of genocide perpetrated against Jews, Romani people, individuals, and others. The tides of war eventually changed in favor of the Allies.

As 1945 began, American and Allied forces made progress in Europe and the Pacific, leading to the downfall of the Axis powers. Joy and profound relief have spread across America when news arrived in May about Germany's surrender. Despite this victory, the Pacific War continued to rage on. It was only in August 1945, when atomic bombs devastated Hiroshima and Nagasaki, that Japan finally surrendered, bringing an end to World War II.

These bombings with weapons unleashed a whole new era of nuclear power that the world still grapples with today. The initial thrill of victory was overshadowed by the realization of the destructive capability that humanity now possessed. It was a moment that raised an urgent question: How should we responsibly manage the power to annihilate life as we know it?

Upon their return, millions of servicemen known as the "G.I.

Generation" or "Greatest Generation" were welcomed back home with parades and tears of joy. But their transition back to life was not without its difficulties. Many experienced psychological wounds, referred to today as PTSD. Known then as "shell shock" or "battle fatigue." Their stories exemplify the spirit of humans in the face of unimaginable trauma.

For groups such as women and minorities, the war's end brought about a complex mix of progress, setbacks, and stagnation. Women were often dismissed from their jobs as men returned, representing a step toward advancing gender equality ideas. Yet this period also planted seeds for feminist movements. The war had provided a taste of parity. It left an indelible impression.

For African Americans specifically, the war's conclusion carried expectations that their sacrifices would lead to advancements in civil rights. The "Double V Campaign" emerged from a sense of hope representing two victories: one against fascism on the soil and the other against discrimination within the country. However, the struggle was far from being resolved. The post-war period served as a crucible for shaping the Civil Rights Movement, fueled by the contradictions faced by those fighting for freedom abroad while experiencing rights denial at home.

Native Americans and Mexican Americans experienced similar narratives. Despite their significant contributions to the war effort, they faced discriminatory barriers that did not immediately dissolve; they discovered that their significant contributions to the war effort did not immediately dismantle discriminatory barriers. Nonetheless, their wartime roles sowed seeds of change that gradually sprouted into movements seeking recognition and rights over subsequent decades.

World War II acted as a turning point that reshaped dynamics. The United States emerged as a superpower and played a pivotal role in designing the post-war world order. This newfound responsibility led the nation into the depths of the Cold War conflicts in Korea and Vietnam and engagements in lands. At the same time, being hailed as the "Arsenal of Democracy" for saving humanity from tyranny, this victory came at a cost that continued to shape our world long after guns ceased to fire.

The legacies of World War II are diverse, encompassing advancements in technology and notable shifts in dynamics. Importantly, it taught us a valuable lesson that continues to hold: freedom is delicate, and we must be watchful and brave and work together as a united community irrespective of our race, gender, or beliefs.

Economic considerations: From the Great Depression to WWII

Challenges and global dynamics

The 1930s were not just a time of economic hardship; they were years that profoundly impacted American society. The Great Depression was like as a storm casting a gray shadow over the vibrant colors of the Roaring Twenties. The stock market crash in 1929 went beyond being an economic downturn; it was an earthquake that shook the nation to its core.

To truly grasp the extent of despair, envision entire families being forced out of their homes with their belongings piled up on sidewalks. Picture the "Okies" farmers displaced by the Dust Bowl embarking on journeys along Route 66 not for adventure but for survival, desperately seeking any kind of work available. The lines of individuals waiting outside soup kitchens stretched across the land like elongated shadows.

A desolate urban street portrait during the Great Depression, portraying the dire circumstances faced by familie

It wasn't about money; it encompassed the loss of dignity, purpose, and hope. In this environment, President Franklin D. Roosevelt's victory in the 1932 election brought a glimmer of hope. His commitment to a "New Deal" went beyond being policy; it symbolized a pact with the American people. The government, once distant, became an active partner in their daily struggles. It was astonishing for citizens to witness government employees contacting directly to offer assistance, create job opportunities, and restore dignity.

The programs initiated under the New Deal, such as the Civilian Conservation Corps (CCC) and Works Progress Administration (WPA), provided needed relief for a wounded nation. They constructed enduring bridges, parks, and buildings still in use today, and more importantly, they reconstructed shattered lives. However, the New Deal also stirred controversy as some believed it exceeded its limits while others felt it didn't go enough. Ultimately, it reflected a nation grappling with self-definition.

Now, one might question why these domestic events held global significance. Here's the crucial point: during the 1930s, economic policies among nations were interconnected like falling dominos. When one faltered, others experienced instability well.

Let's step into a world stage filled with turmoil. In the background, authoritarian leaders emerged, driven by instability and national resentment. Their narratives were dangerous yet enticing in their simplicity; they offered someone to blame and promised to restore pride. Unfortunately, the world had failed to learn a lesson from WWI: imposing punitive peace doesn't foster harmony; instead, it sows the seeds of future conflicts.

Initially, as fascism gained ground in Europe and militarism escalated in Japan, the U.S. clung to isolationism. But history has a way of pulling reluctant players into its grasp. The devastating attack on Pearl Harbor in 1941 served as a wake-up call—a piercing siren that made it clear that the U.S. Could no longer isolate itself from global issues.

During WWII, the American economy experienced a resurgence. The war effort ended the Great Depression as factories buzzed with activity and unemployment rates dropped significantly. Yet this transformation wasn't about improving statistics; it represented a shift in self-perception. The U.S., beyond safeguarding democracy, was also demonstrating its resilience on its home front.

The rise of totalitarian regimes

If we compare the Depression to a global economic storm, it's fair to say that policymakers and decision-makers in the 1930s were navigating uncharted waters. Take, for instance, the Smoot Hawley Tariff Act of 1930. Although its original intention was to safeguard industry, it constricted international trade like a tightening noose. In response, other nations raised their tariffs, causing further tightening of the global economy and subsequent downward spiraling.

Across the Atlantic Ocean, economic instability created fertile ground for dangerous ideologies to take root. It is worth contemplating how desperate circumstances drove people in Germany towards leaders like Hitler, who offered scapegoats for their suffering along with visions of national glory being restored. Similar promises propelled individuals such as Mussolini in Italy and Franco in Spain into positions of power.

They resembled magicians exuding an aura of strength and order amidst the chaos. In moments of desperation, people clung to these illusions, seeking solace.

We must not overlook the involvement of Eastern players in this narrative. With its economic and social challenges, Japan turned to militarism and imperialism to address resource scarcity. These actions were not isolated incidents but rather part of a surge of authoritarianism fueled by economic despair and further ignited by failed peace initiatives following World War I.

The United States, dealing with its economic hardships, initially chose to look the other way. The Neutrality Acts enacted in the 1930s aimed at avoiding getting entangled in quagmires. Nevertheless, history proved to be a teacher emphasizing the interconnected nature of the global community. It became clear that it was not about economics but also about shared human values, freedoms, and rights – principles threatened by the rising tide of darkness in Europe and Asia.

Franklin D. Roosevelt comprehended this reality entirely. His Quarantine Speech delivered in 1937 was more than a plea for moral responsibility; it acknowledged an indisputable truth: no matter America's might or resources, it couldn't erect barriers high enough to isolate itself from the world troubles.

The United States felt the ripple effects of wars and political instability from distant lands. When World War II began in Europe, the U.S. still grappled with its compass and strategic interests. The Lend-Lease Act of 1941 played a role as it allowed support for Allied forces without direct involvement. Yes, history has taught us some lessons; the unexpected attack on Pearl Harbor in December 1941 was a brutal reminder. It shattered any remaining illusions of detachment from global conflicts.

The entry of the United States into WWII marked a turning point. The factories falling silent during the Great Depression now roared back to life. Seeing tanks and airplanes rolling off production lines once dedicated to manufacturing cars and household appliances. Let's not forget about the women workers, famously known as "Rosie the Riveters", who stepped into traditionally male roles, forever changing the workforce landscape. The economy wasn't just bouncing back; it was transforming to meet new global realities and responsibilities.

Cusp in human history

The war's conclusion in 1945 ushered in an era of economic prosperity for America. Why did this happen? Well, imagine a runner trained at altitudes returning to compete at sea level. Unlike Europe and Asia, devastated by war, the United States had its industrial infrastructure intact and significantly improved. The factories that once produced weapons and supplies were now free to manufacture consumer goods, fulfilling a growing demand for everything, from automobiles to refrigerators.

The economic boom was just one aspect of the overall situation. Another critical factor was the landscape. The traditional European powers had diminished influence, while the United

States and the Soviet Union emerged as superpowers. The Bretton Woods Conference in 1944 had already established the U.S. dollar as the primary reserve currency, showcasing America's newfound economic strength. The responsibility and authority that came with being considered the hub of the world was epic!

Furthermore, World War II had spurred technological advancements. Nuclear energy, jet aircraft, synthetic materials, and even the ominous atomic bomb were among many innovations that would shape our world. The United States played a role in these developments and stood at the forefront of this new era of technology.

However, along with prosperity and power come their set of challenges. The United States was responsible for maintaining post-war peace and leading international efforts to rebuild nations devastated by war. The Marshall Plan was an initiative to restore European economic stability and prevent communism from spreading further. It indicated that America's foreign policy had become intricately intertwined with its financial strategy. During this period, many people saw the start of what they called the "American Dream". Thanks to the G.I. Bill, soldiers returning from war could buy homes and attend college, significantly increasing social mobility. Suburbs grew rapidly, universities expanded campuses, and a new middle class emerged. Nevertheless, it's important to note that not everyone had access to this dream, especially marginalized groups facing systemic disparities based on race, gender, and economic status. These inequalities foreshadowed the struggles that would later arise and reach a boiling point.

The United States' rise as a superpower following World War II set the stage for the Cold War—an extended battle for geopolitical dominance that shaped international relations throughout the rest of the 20th century. Let's save that story for the next chapter.

It's worth considering how the same economic and political forces that caused despair in the 1930s ultimately paved the way for a new global order with the United States at its helm. The United States, hesitant about international involvement, now greatly influenced the world stage.

VI

POST-WAR ERA TO PRESENT

11

The Cold War and Its Impact on American Society (1946–1991)

Early Cold War, Civil Rights, and Socio-Political Movements 1946–1975

Origins of the Cold War

As the embers of World War II slowly diminished, a new conflict with ideologies began to emerge. It was like two colossal giants locked in a stare-down, both refusing to back down while simultaneously fearing the dire consequences of confrontation. These giants represent none other than the United States and the Soviet Union – two superpowers with vastly different visions for the world.

In 1947, President Truman announced a pivotal policy known as the Truman Doctrine, which promised support to nations facing threats from Communism. It drew a line in the sand against Soviet expansionism.

Why did this sudden change transform former wartime allies into bitter adversaries? After World War II, the alliances formed during the war started to weaken, revealing ideological differences between the United States and the Soviet Union. While they had worked together to defeat the Axis Powers, their post-war visions for the world were fundamentally divergent. The United States, rooted in its belief in democracy and a capitalist economy, envisioned a world that reflected these values. On the other hand, the Soviet Union, with its authoritarian rule and state-controlled system, aimed to spread its version of Communism. This clash of ideologies went beyond economic or governance issues; it represented a clash of worldviews regarding concepts like freedom, control, and which direction nations worldwide should take in their future endeavors.

The late 1940s and early 1950s witnessed the spread of what came to be known as the "Cold War" This term is fitting because although direct conflict between the two superpowers was avoided mainly, their rivalry was tangible through wars, espionage activities, and an intense nuclear arms race. Think of it like a game of chess with high stakes. Both players carefully position their pieces to exert influence without confronting each other. This strategic maneuvering and indirect competition characterized the relationship between the United States and the Soviet Union during the Cold War.

As these giants engaged in a battle of wills, America experienced significant domestic transformations in the late 1950s and 1960s. This period was marked by social unrest. Figures like Martin Luther King Jr., a leader, spearheaded the Civil Rights Movement, which aimed to challenge systemic racial segregation and discrimination. Reflect on a world where your skin color determined where you could eat, which seat you could take on a bus, or which water fountain you could use. The fight against these injustices became a defining battle in America's history, spotlighting the nation's values.

While the Civil Rights Movement was making waves, another movement was brewing behind the scenes. Led by trailblazers like Betty Friedan, the Feminist Movement emerged to challenge gender roles and advocate for women's rights. Picture a world where women, who had long been confined to roles, now bravely demanded equality in workplaces, politics, and society.

But as these movements gained momentum, another significant event loomed large: the Vietnam War. The jungles of
Vietnam became the backdrop for America's endeavor to curb
Communism in Southeast Asia. However, this conflict quickly
became entangled in controversy and opposition as many
questioned its morality and purpose. The sight of men being
drafted and sent off to fight in a distant land ignited nationwide
protests and deep divisions.

Would America prioritize its commitment to fighting Communism over addressing pressing issues at home? This tension
between threats and internal challenges came to symbolize
the era. As we navigate through these times, it's important to
remember that the people who lived during this period were
not passive bystanders. They were participants with their
dreams, fears, and aspirations. They enjoyed dancing to Elvis's
music and found inspiration in JFK's vision of a "New Frontier"
And marched for peace, justice, and freedom. Together, the
actions of Americans from all walks of life played a role in
reshaping the nation's society.

1970s Socio-political movements

Against the backdrop of the Cold War's influence, the Civil
Rights Movement faced its unique obstacles and challenges.

While historical achievements such as the Civil Rights Act of
1964 and the Voting Rights Act of 1965 were steps forward, it is
crucial to recognize that they did not instantaneously eradicate

racial discrimination. In some areas, there were instances of race riots that erupted due to frustrations surrounding economic disparities and police brutality. Just envision the heart-wrenching scenes of cities like Detroit and Los Angeles engulfed in flames, where anger and despair were palpable. These events served as a reminder that although laws could be changed, shifting hearts and minds often required more time.

At the same time, the Chicano Movement emerged to advocate for the rights of Mexican Americans, who also sought their share of the dream. Let your imagination wander into a world where individuals divided by language and culture find ground in their shared aspirations for a brighter future. Moreover, it is essential to acknowledge the Native American rights movement symbolized by significant events like the occupation of Alcatraz Island, which aimed at reclaiming lost lands and asserting their rights. Picture in your mind's eye the sight of indigenous people standing steadfast on a rock in San Francisco Bay demanding justice—people whose ancestors once roamed freely across this vast continent.

As these movements gained momentum, so did resistance against the Vietnam War. College campuses became hotbeds for war sentiment—a sentiment tragically exemplified by events like the Kent State shootings in 1970. This was a time when young individuals, who were not much older than school graduates, fearlessly challenged the power of their government. At the time, there was a growing awareness of environmental issues due in part to Rachel Carson's influential book, "Silent Spring". People started realizing that the conveniences of life came at a price – the well-being of our planet. Additionally, these years saw the emergence of the LGBTQ rights movement, symbolized by the Stonewall riots in 1969. It was a moment when an oppressed and marginalized community defiantly sought acceptance and equality. These domestic struggles, Even though intense, still unfolded under the overarching shadow of the Cold War. Despite diplomatic improvements, events like the Cuban Missile Crisis reminded everyone that there was always a threat of nuclear devastation hanging over the world.

Understanding that this period in America's history wasn't about policies, laws, or international relations is crucial. It was about individuals – like a young American girl bravely enrolling in an all-white school or a gay couple openly holding hands for the first time in public. These were people, with their own stories, who shaped this era.

The convergence of the Cold War and various social movements

In this era, numerous socio-political movements brought concerns to the forefront of American society. Yet, it is essential to note that the Cold War remained a preoccupation for policymakers and the general public. This ideological struggle seemed to permeate every aspect of life, from elections to popular culture.

Imagine yourself as an American in the mid-1970s. As you watch the evening news, you might see reports suggesting a thawing of relations through détente with the Soviet Union. At the time, there would be disheartening revelations surfacing from the Watergate scandal that shake your trust in government institutions.

In 1972, the United States and the Soviet Union signed the Strategic Arms Limitation Treaty (SALT I), signaling both nations' recognition of the dangers of an escalating nuclear arms race and bringing a ray of hope during tense Cold War relations. However, amidst these global developments, America had its internal challenges. The end of the Vietnam War 1975, marked by the Fall of Saigon, brought relief. It also prompted deep introspection. People wondered about the accomplishments of the conflict and whether the sacrifices in terms of lives and resources were genuinely worthwhile.

During this period, there were also hurdles to overcome. The 1973 oil crisis caused by OPEC's oil embargo resulted in queues at gas stations and sparked discussions about America's dependence on foreign oil. Conceive how frustrating it must have been for families planning summer road trips only to be confronted with fuel shortages.

By the mid-1970s, there was progress made by the feminist movement as well. The fight for gender equality through initiatives like the Equal Rights Amendment (even though it was never ratified) symbolized a struggle for women's rights. Picture conversations around family dinner tables where traditional roles were being questioned and redefined. At the time, the counterculture movement, represented by the hippies of the 1960s, started to fade away, giving way to a growing sense of skepticism and a shift toward conservatism. The country was going through a period of change, trying to find its balance.

As this era ended, Martin Luther King Jr.'s words resonated deeply: "The arc of the moral universe is long, but it bends toward justice". America experienced transformations over three decades, both domestically and internationally. The nation confronted challenges, celebrated triumphs, and always strived for a 'more perfect union'.

The Conclusion of the Cold War, Emergence of Social Movements and Environmentalism 1976–1991

End of the Cold War

The late 1970s and 1980s in America resembled the scenes of a thrilling play as individuals grappled with past decisions while confronting a newfound understanding of global realities.

Illustration of an American city during the 1980s, capturing the socio-political essence of the era

In 1979, the United States faced the Iranian hostage crisis, where 52 American diplomats were held captive for 444 days. Additionally, the Soviet Union's invasion of Afghanistan the same year signaled that the Cold War was far from over. Amidst escalating tensions, a remarkable transformation was unfolding within America. The nation experienced an awakening regarding concerns—an acknowledgment fueled by visible environmental degradation and notable incidents such as the Three Mile Island nuclear accident in 1979. A growing awareness developed that the Earth's resources were not limitless. Imagine a family embracing recycling for the first time or communities uniting for beach clean-ups. The prevailing mindset of the era shifted from consumption to thoughtful conservation.

In the 1980s, Ronald Reagan assumed the presidency, bringing with him a clear opposition to Communism and a promise to revive the American spirit following a perceived period of decline. His economic policies, commonly known as "Reaganomics", emphasized tax reductions, deregulation, and cuts in government spending. Some saw this era as a time of prosperity and renewed national pride, but it was also criticized for widening economic disparities.

Amidst the political landscape, popular culture thrived. Michael Jackson's "Thriller" blared from radios while movies like "E.T." and "The Breakfast Club" captured people's imaginations. As in previous eras, art and entertainment reflected reality and avenues for escapism.

Undoubtedly, Reagan's firm approach towards the USSR, epitomized by his famous call to "tear down this wall!" laid the groundwork for significant geopolitical transformations. However, as he increased defense spending and introduced the Strategic Defense Initiative (often called "Star Wars"), many Americans and people worldwide held their breath, questioning whether these actions would bring the world closer to a conflict.

Nevertheless, amidst these tensions, communication channels were opening up. In the latter part of the 1980s, Mikhail Gorbachev's policies of "glasnost" (meaning openness) and "perestroika" (meaning restructuring) indicated a potential shift in relations between the Soviet Union and America.

As we approached the end of the 1980s, America faced a profound crisis: the AIDS epidemic. This deeply misunder-stood and heavily stigmatized disease claimed countless lives, particularly within the LGBTQ+ community. The epidemic exposed deeply rooted societal biases and highlighted the government's initial reluctance and delay in addressing the burgeoning health crisis. But it also sparked a movement where communities came together to support patients and advocate for advancements.

Dissolution of the Soviet Union

As the 1990s arrived, the world stood on the brink of witnessing the end of the Cold War. Seeing the crumbling of symbols representing that era was genuinely astonishing for many who grew up fearing nuclear destruction.

Think of the streets of Berlin in November 1989. The once-divided East and West Berliners separated by the Berlin Wall now climbed atop it together, chipping away pieces as souvenirs and embracing their loved ones. Reagan's famous words urging Gorbachev to "tear down this wall" were not just symbolic; they became a reality.

What were the reasons behind this monumental event? A combination of internal economic struggles, a longing for freedom in Eastern Europe, and Gorbachev's reforms played a significant role. However, it was indeed the spirit of the people. Exemplified by protests like Leipzig's Monday demonstrations. That significantly hastened its end. As America witnessed the unraveling of the Soviet Union, it concurrently grappled with the controversial 'War on Drugs,' a policy that had profound and long-lasting social and economic consequences, particularly in communities of color. The crack epidemic and subsequent "War on Drugs" intensified during this period. This led to rates of incarceration, particularly affecting Black and Latino communities. As some parts of our country turned into battle zones on our streets, communities were torn apart – laying down the foundations for debates around criminal justice even today.

Alongside these developments, there was a glimmer of hope regarding environmental consciousness. Earth Day, which began in 1970, gained participation and support. People of all ages, including children, expressed concerns about deforestation, the need for oceans, and the urgent fight against climate change. Although it may seem like a detail in the enormous scope of history, the controversy surrounding the protection of the spotted owl became symbolic of the ongoing conflict between environmental preservation and economic interests during that era.

During the 1980s and early 1990s, Indigenous movements experienced a resurgence. The lasting effects of injustices such as broken treaties, forced relocations, and cultural suppression still weighed heavily on communities. In contrast, events like "The Longest Walk 2" in 1988 brought renewed attention to rights and environmental protection efforts—pushing for recognition and justice.

In parallel with these developments, pop culture continued its changing role as both a reflection of societal concerns and an escape from them. The rise of hip-hop as a force in music mirrored urban realities. Television series like "A Different World" and "Roseanne" directly confronted societal norms and initiated essential conversations within American households. Additionally, shows such as "The Fresh Prince of Bel-Air" blended humor with moments touching social issues and challenging certain stereotypes.

Global consequences

December 25, 1991, was a turning point in global dynamics. Mikhail Gorbachev, who led the USSR, officially declared the end of the Soviet Union. This announcement marked the conclusion of the Cold War. Yet, amidst celebrations, new challenges arose in its aftermath. For America, this meant entering a period without an adversary for the first time in decades. The bipolar world had disintegrated and given rise to a new geopolitical landscape.

Initially established as a defense against the USSR, NATO now had to redefine its purpose. Simultaneously, countries under communist rule began their transition towards democracy and capitalism – an undertaking filled with aspirations and uncertainties.

Nevertheless, it is essential to note that late 20th-century history was not solely centered around politics. It was a time when technology rapidly advanced, completely changing how people lived, worked, and communicated.

What if you're being transported from the 1960s to the 1980s and witnessing the emergence of personal computers? It would be like going from horse-drawn carriages to electric cars! Companies like Microsoft and Apple started gaining prominence, and the idea of an interconnected world began to take shape.

Alongside these advancements, social dynamics were also evolving. Women, who had made progress during the feminist movements of the 1960s and 70s, were now finding their voices in fields traditionally dominated by men. The appointment of Sandra Day O'Connor as the female Supreme Court Justice in 1981 represented this progress. Yet, not all narratives of this era were positive. The worsening AIDS crisis in the 1980s marked the era. While communities came together to provide support and raise awareness, federal authorities still lacked a response, which led to nationwide mobilization efforts and campaigns by groups like ACT UP.

Toward the end of this period, LGBTQ+ community members, who had long been marginalized, began asserting their presence more prominently in mainstream society. Pride parades grew in size, became more daring, and embraced inclusivity, reaching their peak with the 1993 March on Washington, where hundreds of thousands gathered to advocate for rights.

From the tensions of the Cold War to the dawn of the age, from societal changes to the celebration of diversity, this era brought about significant transformations. The stories from this time go beyond world leaders and political choices; they are accounts of communities and individuals who influenced history's path even during uncertain times.

12

Into the 21st Century: Challenges and Changes (1992–Present)

Advancements and the Information Age 1992–2000

American life in the digital era

The '90s, a decade filled with memories of Y2K, Tamagotchis, grunge music, and vibrant windbreakers, also witnessed technology and the internet shaping lives in unprecedented ways. Take a moment to envision a world without the internet. It's pretty challenging. Yet before the '90s, very few households had access to an internet connection. But by the end of that decade, the World Wide Web seemed to be present everywhere.

A depiction of a tech store in the 1990s, filled with people eagerly exploring the latest gadgets.

Let's go back to 1994 when Netscape introduced Navigator—an influential web browser that popularized internet browsing for many. Can you recall that sound of a dial-up modem? The anticipation building up as you waited for that connection amidst those beeps and static?

The 90s anthem, for many, signaling the era's arrival, was characterized by the simultaneous growth of personal computing; during the 1990s, traditional beige P.C. boxes transformed into sleeker and more powerful machines. Apple caused a stir in 1998 with the introduction of the iMac. It was a computer that represented advanced technology and made a statement with its all-in-one design and colorful translucent casing.

This period also witnessed the emergence of online startups, known as "dot coms", which promised innovative solutions for digital living. The mere mention of a business model attracted substantial investments, turning companies like Webvan, Kozmo, and Pets.com into household names. Many people left their conventional jobs to chase after internet fortunes. Often referred to as the "Gold Rush of the Digital Age". Although every Gold Rush eventually reaches its limits, as we approached the millennium, many dot coms lacked sustainable business models despite their initial buzz. The bubble finally burst in the 2000s, resulting in significant market corrections and reshaping the trajectory of the tech industry.

The 1990s were a mix of significant cultural moments and political changes in America. Bill Clinton's presidency, characterized by prosperity, was also marked by controversies. Television shows like "Friends" and "The X Files" became symbols of popular culture. Hip hop, an underground genre, skyrocketed into the mainstream, with artists such as Tupac Shakur, The Notorious B.I.G., And Dr. Dre becoming influential figures for a whole generation.

While technology and culture flourished during this time, society grappled with issues. The Columbine High School shooting in 1999 sparked debates on gun control, youth culture, and school safety. Natural disasters like the 1994 Northridge earthquake reminded Americans of nature's power.

As the decade ended and people anxiously awaited the start of a new millennium, there was excitement and apprehension. Would computers crash because of the Y2K bug? Bring modern civilization to a halt? Looking back now, it may seem funny. At that time, there was genuine uncertainty. When clocks struck midnight on January 1, 2000, sighs of relief could be heard nationwide. Let's look at the fascinating technological advancements of the 1990s, where we explore the evolution of mobile phones, the growing gaming culture, and how digital tools started reshaping our daily lives.

It was a time when "mobile phone" referred to a device with an external antenna and a battery pack almost as big as a brick. The 90s would soon change that perception. Remember the Nokia 3310 with its pixelated game of Snake? How about the Motorola StarTAC that began the flip phone era? These devices were more than phones; they represented a future where communication would be liberated from landlines.

The rise of phones was just one aspect of a broader communication shift. Email, once considered novel, became a mainstream mode of interaction, allowing messages to travel across continents in seconds. AOL's iconic "You've Got Mail" notification became synonymous with connection and signaled an era.

While phones and emails revolutionized communication, entertainment also changed during this time. Step into the world of video games. While video games had already existed before the 1990s, this decade witnessed their explosion into mainstream pop culture. Sony's PlayStation made its debut, offering stunning games that surpassed anything seen before. Nintendo Game Boy, introduced in 1989, became a symbol of bringing portable gaming to the masses. As a result, both kids and adults from the 90s have memories of trading Pokémon or competing in thrilling "Mario Kart" races.

Not to be outdone, Microsoft made its mark in the tech industry with the release of Windows 95, their operating system at that time. Its launch was monumental. This caused people to camp outside stores overnight. In one swoop, it introduced features such as the Start menu and taskbar that we now consider standard.

Simultaneously, technology was advancing in ways that were not always visible. The Human Genome Project commenced during this decade to map all human genes. This colossal undertaking formed a foundation for future medical, genetics, and biology breakthroughs.

However, amidst progress, there were also controversies during the 1990s. Microsoft was embroiled in an antitrust lawsuit due to accusations of monopolistic practices. As the years passed, it became evident that tech giants were accumulating power, prolonging the legal case. As we arrived at the millennium, people were concerned about the potential Y2K bug and how these technological advancements would impact society. Would we become overly dependent on gadgets? Would our privacy be compromised in this evolving digital age? Despite these concerns, there was also a sense of excitement and curiosity. We stood at the brink of an era where endless possibilities awaited us. In our exploration of the 1990s, it becomes clear that two names. Steve Jobs and Bill Gates. Shine brightly amidst all the marvels that defined this decade.

Media and Titans: Changing Landscapes and Influential Figures

During that time, these influential figures in the technology world, representing Apple and Microsoft, respectively, pushed the boundaries of what computers could achieve. Despite Apple's challenges in the 1980s, Steve Jobs returned to the company in the late 1990s to rebrand Apple as a symbol of elegant design and user-friendly technology. The iMac G3, known for its colors and distinctive design, became an iconic representation of this new era at Apple. Regarding software advancements, the 1990s witnessed the introduction of Mac OS 8 and 9, pivotal releases leading up to macOS as we know it today – a platform that has gained popularity among users.

In the O.S. competition, Bill Gates and Microsoft introduced Windows 98 – a significant upgrade from Windows 95. This new version boasted system performance, seamless internet integration, and broader hardware compatibility.

While these tech giants were competing to surpass each other's achievements, there was also notable transformation within the media industry. Instances such as Disney's acquisition of A.B.C., and separately, Time Warner's merging with Turner Broadcasting and C.B.S.'s allying with Westinghouse indicated a growing trend toward media consolidation as a result of these mergers between players in television radio broadcasting, and film production industries emerged powerful media conglomerates that exerted significant influence, over public discourse and cultural trends.

The 1990s also saw the birth of the home satellite industry, with companies like DirecTV providing an alternative to cable television. By installing a dish on their roofs, households gained access to channels, changing how people watched T.V. Still, perhaps the significant change in media during this time was the emergence of 24-hour news coverage. Channels like CNN delivered real-time reporting, ensuring viewers stayed connected to events worldwide. The Gulf War served as an example of this new style of journalism, captivating millions with live broadcasts from the front lines. Nevertheless, as 24-hour news coverage grew in popularity, it also brought challenges such as media sensationalism. In this competitive landscape, stories needed to be gripping enough to keep audiences engaged, sometimes leading to exaggerated or overly dramatic reporting.

As the 1990s neared its end, there was anticipation and concern over Y2K. This "Millennium Bug" instilled fears of global computer system failures when the calendar flipped from 1999 to 2000. Governments and corporations have invested billions in addressing vulnerabilities. When midnight struck on December 31, 1999, many held their breath in anticipation. As the new millennium commenced, it went smoothly without major issues. The successful mitigation of the Y2K bug showcased humanity's ability to anticipate and collaboratively address substantial technological challenges.

September 11 and its aftermath 2001–2010

9/11

On the morning of September 11, 2001, like any other day, people in the United States were going about their routines. Going to work or school while flights took off to different destinations. Little did they know that this day would leave an enduring mark on history.

A depiction of the chaos and confusion in the streets of New York City after the Twin Towers were hit

Take a moment to imagine the chaos and confusion that engulfed the streets of New York City when two planes crashed into the Twin Towers of the World Trade Center. As smoke filled the air, emergency services hurried to respond without knowing that more horrors were yet to come. Another plane targeted the Pentagon in Arlington, Virginia. Meanwhile, United Flight 93, due to the courageous efforts of its passengers, crashed in a Pennsylvania field before reaching its intended target. On that day, nearly 3,000 innocent lives were tragically taken from us. The essence of the United States, its feeling of invincibility, was shaken. The question "Why?" resounded in the hearts of every American. The answer didn't take long to emerge; a militant group called Al Qaeda, led by Osama bin Laden, claimed responsibility. While the attacks on September 11 were meticulously planned to instill fear in the Western world and seek revenge for perceived injustices in the Middle East, they were rooted in religious extremism.

In an address to the nation, President George W. Bush articulated the American people's pain, anger, and resilience. He stated, "Our cherished way of life and our precious freedom were targeted... But they failed; our nation remains strong". As we mourned as a country, these tragic events also sparked a sense of unity and patriotism among Americans. The iconic Stars and Stripes flew everywhere. From homes to car antennas. As a symbol that we will never forget.

The aftermath of September 11 brought about changes in domestic and foreign policies within the United States. In October 2001, the USA PATRIOT Act was signed into law to enhance law enforcement surveillance capabilities to prevent attacks. However, this legislation also sparked discussions regarding liberties as critics argued that it compromised individual rights in the name of security.

On a scale, these attacks triggered the U.S.-led War on Terror. Initially, Afghanistan became the focus due to its connection with Al Qaeda. The United States and its allies launched "Operation Enduring Freedom" to dismantle Al Qaeda and remove the Taliban from power.

While the Taliban regime was swiftly overthrown, the conflict persisted. The complexities of politics in Afghanistan's challenging terrain and the resurgence of Taliban fighters prolonged efforts to establish a stable and democratic Afghanistan. Nevertheless, it is essential to note that Afghanistan was not the theater in this War on Terror. The narrative surrounding threats posed by weapons of mass destruction (W.M.D.) soon shifted attention toward Iraq and its leader, Saddam Hussein.

While the focus of America's attention remained on Afghanistan in early 2002, there were growing signs of a broader conflict on the horizon. President George W. Bush's use of the term "Axis of Evil" during his State of the Union address drew attention to North Korea, Iran, and Iraq as countries that posed threats to global peace. Out of these three countries, Iraq became the concern. The U.S. Government claimed that Saddam Hussein's regime possessed weapons of mass destruction (W.M.D.'s) and connected with terrorist organizations like Al Qaeda. These claims, which were later proven to be primarily unfounded and controversial, served as the basis for the invasion of Iraq in 2003.

One can think of the tension within diplomatic circles during this time. The United Nations Security Council was deeply divided over whether or not to go to War. While the United States and the United Kingdom advocated for action against Iraq, other member nations, such as France and Germany, expressed skepticism.

The absence of a United Nations mandate for engaging in war resulted in protests worldwide, some of which were among the largest in history. But on March 20, 2003, the action commenced. The display of missiles and bombs illuminated the night sky over Baghdad. The military strategy employed was known as "Shock and Awe" aiming to hinder Iraq's military capabilities and lower morale. On April 9, U.S. Troops entered Baghdad, marking the beginning of Saddam Hussein's downfall.

It may seem logical to assume that overthrowing a dictator would bring peace; however, Iraq's experience unfolded differently. With Saddam's removal from power, various ethnic and sectarian groups suppressed under his iron-fisted rule sought to assert their influence and authority. Consequently, the nation found itself embroiled in a war.

Back in the United States, public opinion began to shift. Debates intensified due to the lack of weapons of mass destruction (W.M.D.'s) being found and the increasing number of American casualties. The costs incurred by this War—human lives lost and economic burdens—became points of contention within U.S. Politics. As time passed, the initial goal shifted from disarming Saddam to building an Iraq through nation-building efforts.

The Financial Collapse and the Great Recession

Beyond the battle zones, the impact of this War on Terror resonated on a global scale. Imagine this scenario: You've been working hard to save money for your dream house, considered the epitome of the American Dream. With property values on a constant upward trajectory and attractive loan options available, you gather the courage to make the big purchase. Yet, before you know it, the value of your acquired home drastically declines quickly. Many homeowners found themselves in a situation where they owed more on their mortgages than the value of their homes. This was not a story of a few individuals but a widespread issue affecting millions.

The economic downturn in 2008, often referred to as the 'Great Recession' significantly exacerbated this problem. It all began with signs of trouble in the subprime mortgage market back in 2007. Financial institutions had been granting loans to individuals with less-than-ideal credit scores, relying on the belief that housing prices would continue to rise. When homeowners started defaulting on their loans, it triggered a chain reaction that led to consequences.

Familiar names like Lehman Brothers, Merrill Lynch, and Bear Stearns faced their crises one after another. Lehman Brothers' bankruptcy in September 2008 had far-reaching effects on the global financial system. The stock market experienced a decline, credit became scarce, and consumer confidence took a hit.

The U.S. Congress passed, and the President signed, the Emergency Economic Stabilization Act of 2008 to address the freezing credit market and its implications. This act established a program of $700 billion aimed at purchasing troubled bank assets. This decision sparked debates over whether it was an intervention or merely an undeserved bailout for Wall Street's risky behavior.

It's important to note that this crisis wasn't limited to America; it profoundly impacted the global financial system. With interconnected banks facing solvency issues and stock markets plummeting across countries, international trade also experienced significant declines. Regardless of their economic strength, countries worldwide grappled with challenges like rising unemployment, declining consumer confidence, and contracting economies. In the United States, the recession exposed societal issues. The unemployment rate peaked at 10% in 2009, the highest since the 1980s. Many people experienced foreclosures on their homes, retirement savings vanished, and numerous dreams were put on hold or shattered. On the other hand, with every crisis comes an opportunity for introspection. It raised questions about whether the relentless pursuit of profit had contributed to this situation and if regulations were too lenient.

In the years following the recession, there were efforts to reform regulations. The Dodd-Frank Wall Street Reform and Consumer Protection Act of 2010 aimed to mitigate risks in the system. The public's trust in both institutions and government was shaken, leading to movements like Occupy Wall Street that criticized wealth inequality and corporate influence in politics.

Although the 2000s concluded with turbulence, they exemplified the world's complexities. As America navigated its role in politics, economics, and society, it became evident that decisions made within its borders had far-reaching consequences beyond its shores.

Contemporary era 2011–2023

Picture yourself stepping into a time machine in the 1960s and finding yourself in 2011. The world would feel unfamiliar with touchscreen phones, online communities, and instant communication dominating the scene. The cultural and technological changes during that time were immense. However, beneath this surface, America was still grappling with timeless issues.

A 2021 remote work setting representing the shift to work-from-home culture

Equality, rights, justice, and the environment were at the center of debates. While these topics were not new, their context had evolved. Let's consider the fight for LGBTQ+ rights as an example. In 2015, when Obergefell v. Hodges legalized same-sex marriage across the United States through a landmark Supreme Court decision, it marked a triumph. Yet this victory was built upon decades of activism. This shift reflected an acceptance within society even though some still opposed it. Alongside these discussions, there was also a contemplation of the existential issue of climate change. As the decade progressed, we witnessed rising sea levels, record-breaking temperatures, and devastating natural disasters, adding urgency to the conversation. The Paris Agreement 2015 offered hope as nations came together to address crises collectively. But still, some young activists felt immediate action was necessary and believed America should take the lead.

While these debates were happening, Silicon Valley quietly shaped the future. Tech giants such as Apple, Google, Amazon, and Facebook have impacted our daily lives. We could order food, find a date, watch movies, or even participate in protests with smartphones. Additionally, as Uncle Ben once told Peter Parker, "With great power, traditionally, comes great responsibility". The question remained: Was Silicon Valley prepared to shoulder that responsibility?

The truth was that as technology became intertwined with every aspect of our lives, new challenges emerged. The spread of news became an issue, along with concerns about data privacy and screen addiction. These very platforms that connected people also had the consequence of dividing them by creating echo chambers and reinforcing biases.

Let's pause for a moment. Imagine ourselves sitting at a coffee shop back in 2013. To your left, two young women are conversing about the latest episode of a popular Netflix series they've been streaming on their devices. On your right, a man enthusiastically shares his plans for an app he is developing, convinced that it will impact the world. Meanwhile, you take a sip of your latte conveniently ordered through an app and marvel at how things are evolving.

Brace yourself because the pace is about to accelerate even further.

Disruption

It was a time of change that affected traditional norms and established institutions. This decade-plus span witnessed the accelerated transformation from politics to technology and social justice movements to concerns.

Being a teenager in 2011? It may have been you, your little brother or sister. The internet wasn't new or exciting; it had become integral to our lives. Social media platforms like Twitter, Facebook, Instagram, and later TikTok were no longer places to share photos; they became powerful tools for self-expression and activism. As we grew into adulthood by 2023, the world around us transformed.

The Impact of Social Media on society went beyond simply sharing moments. Platforms like Twitter, Facebook, Instagram, and the newer addition TikTok became day public squares where movements were born and campaigns were led. They provided a voice for those historically silenced. For instance, the #BlackLivesMatter movement emerged in 2013. Shed light on systemic racism, leading to nationwide protests and international solidarity.

Similarly, movements such as #MeToo sparked conversations about harassment that reshaped societal attitudes and workplace policies. These platforms also presented challenges. The rapid spread of misinformation influenced opinions and even affected election outcomes. Consequently, efforts to monitor and control this deluge of data became vital.

The political landscape in America changed with deepening polarization. The 2016 presidential election brought a victory for Donald Trump fueled by a populist wave and a rejection of traditional political norms. Throughout his presidency, controversies, policy shifts, and a distinct style of governance marked his tenure.

In contrast, the 2020 election saw Joe Biden elected as president, promising unity and a return to conventional diplomatic practices. The political divide seemed more pronounced than ever before as debates on critical issues such as healthcare and gun control intensified.

In science and innovation, there was renewed enthusiasm for space exploration. Companies like SpaceX and Blue Origin took the lead in making space travel and the possibility of establishing human colonies on Mars seem less like fiction and more like achievable goals. Successful launches alongside projects like the Starlink satellite constellation became milestones in commercial space travel.

A teenager named Greta Thunberg from Sweden sparked a youth movement demanding action against climate change. Her solitary protest grew into Fridays for Future" demonstrations. Young people challenged established institutions in America and advocated for a sustainable future. The Paris Agreement 2015 aimed to unite nations to address climate change challenges. The US initially withdrew from the agreement under President Trump but later rejoined under President Biden, signaling a renewed commitment to environmental concerns.

Changes in society were also prominent during this time. In 2015, the U.S. Supreme Court ruled in Obergefell v. Hodges, guaranteeing equal marriage rights for same-sex couples in all states.

COVID-19

The year 2019 can be described as nothing short of a "game changer". Just as the world rejoiced at the beginning of a decade, an unseen adversary emerged from obscurity. COVID 19, an entirely new coronavirus strain.

When reports first surfaced from Wuhan, China, about this virus, very few could have anticipated its immense transformative effects that were soon to follow. In March 2020, the World Health Organization announced that we faced a pandemic that completely changed our lives. Can you recall where you were when everything suddenly came to a halt? Busy streets turned into ghost towns. Offices, schools, theaters, and gyms shut down. Face masks, previously primarily seen in hospitals, became an item. We started suspecting every cough or sneeze. Social distancing became normal.

Amidst this isolation, technology proved its strength. Zoom meetings replaced gatherings. Distant families found ways to connect through video calls. Doctors started seeing patients via telemedicine. Students adapted to e-learning methods. Working from home went from being a luxury to becoming a necessity.

Despite all the conveniences technology brought during this time, the pandemic also exposed societal inequalities. Not everyone had the privilege of working or accessing online education quickly. Frontline workers, underpaid and under-valued, risked their lives daily on behalf of others. The debate surrounding healthcare. It is a contentious issue in America. Reached new heights.

On a scale beyond our personal lives, nations faced numer-ous challenges as well; economies took a hit; supply chains were disrupted; political tensions escalated, and finding a vaccine became not only about battling the virus but also about geopolitical rivalries. However, a new debate emerged when vaccines were finally developed in record time. That of fairness and distribution in vaccine access. It's pretty fascinating. Humanity's collective vulnerabilities and strengths came to the forefront in the face of an enemy. While the virus didn't discriminate among people, our responses often showcased disparities. It became a test of our resilience, adaptability, and unity. Some excelled while others struggled.

While the world grappled with this health crisis, technology continued its advancement. The seeds of a revolution were being planted—artificial intelligence (A.I.). Siri, Alexa, and

Google Assistant transformed from tools into integral parts of households.

The question was whether we were prepared for this world where machines could think, learn, and predict outcomes. As A.I. made strides in healthcare, finance, entertainment, and even the creative arts, concerns about job displacement, ethical dilemmas, and data privacy emerged. Would AI be our savior or our competitor? Perhaps it could be both? Only time would provide us with the answers.

Artificial intelligence

By the 2020s, A.I. had evolved from a mere topic of discussion in tech labs to a tangible reality that influenced various aspects of our daily lives. Machines were not capable of "thinking", "learning", and even "creating", but they also raised significant ethical questions.

One pressing concern was determining liability when accidents involving AI-powered cars occurred. Additionally, as A.I. began to play a role in diagnosing diseases, what would happen if it made an error? Another question arose when AI-generated articles, music, and art emerged: who owned the rights to these creations?

Amidst these inquiries, there was also a sense of awe. In medicine, A.I. systems demonstrated accuracy in scanning and diagnosing certain conditions, surpassing human doctors in some cases. Financial industries utilized A.I. to predict market trends while algorithms composed music and aided in design and filmmaking within the arts realm.

The American job market experienced shifts as well. While specific jobs became obsolete due to advancements in A.I. technology, new opportunities emerged in fields such as data analysis, programming, and ethics. Recognizing the changing landscape, students enthusiastically enrolled in universities offering courses centered around A.I. However, along with our reliance on technology, we also became aware of the vulnerabilities it brought. Cybersecurity emerged as a concern, leading nations to strengthen their digital defenses while dealing with attempts by rogue entities to exploit them. Amidst these concerns, a significant debate arose regarding the essence of humanity. Were we sacrificing the qualities that define us as human beings in our relentless pursuit of progress? Was there a line that machines should not cross?

Let's take a moment to see ourselves sitting in our living rooms in 2023. We have an AI-powered device that controls the temperature, suggests recipes tailored to our needs, and even plays music composed specifically for us. It seems like something out of a science fiction novel. It's real. Integrating technology into our physical lives is now seamless, yet we still face the challenge of understanding and managing the immense power at our disposal.

13

Eternal Echoes

As we find ourselves standing on the brink of the pages within this book, gazing out into the expanse of time we have traversed, a profound realization dawns upon us: History is more than just a collection of dates, figures, and events. It is a woven tapestry intricately crafted with threads of human ambition, dreams, struggles, and resilience. The story of the

United States is one pattern within this grand design. Yet, it holds valuable lessons and inspiring moments that cause us to contemplate deeply the essence of human existence.

From the communities that first called this land their home to the brave settlers who ventured across oceans in search of new horizons to the visionary individuals who have reshaped our society in modern times – each era in American history provides us with a glimpse into the very soul of humanity. Our journey has taught us that nations are not merely boundaries on a map or political entities; they are living organisms that constantly evolve, grow, and sometimes stumble.

The tale of America does not boast unfaltering perfection. Instead, it tells a narrative of conflicts, contradictions, and challenges. However, at its core lies a testament to the indomitable spirit present within every human being.

A spirit that resisted tyranny, striving for equality in the face of discrimination and exploring the realms of the known and unknown both on Earth and beyond.

As we conclude this chapter and reflect, let us not simply inquire, "What have we discovered about America?" Instead, contemplate, "What have we discovered about ourselves?" History's cyclical nature teaches us that while circumstances may change our fundamental human desires, fears and aspirations remain constant.

This journey serves as a reminder that societal progress is not always linear. There are peaks of accomplishment and valleys of despair. Yet, during the most challenging moments when uncertainty clouds our way like dense fog, the essence of our human story lies in pushing forward. It is fueled by a curiosity for knowledge, an enduring hunger for a better tomorrow, and an unwavering hope in every human heart.

Perhaps the profound realization is the impermanence of it all. Nations and civilizations fall while current times continue to flow ceaselessly. So you may ask yourself, what is the purpose behind it all? Maybe it isn't about reaching a destination but embracing the journey itself.

It's all about the stories we create, the legacies we leave behind, and the lasting impact of our actions that reverberate throughout time.

As you finish reading this book, may you gain knowledge and wisdom, understand the strength of diversity, value empathy over judgment, and recognize the potential when people unite to pursue a shared vision?

Our journey through America's history is more than an account of a nation; it's a contemplation of humanity's timeless pursuit. Seeking meaning, purpose, and our place in the vast cosmic symphony of existence.

We often say that history is written by those who triumph. Remember that we are each victorious in our own unique way. Every day, we live, breathe, dream, and take action; we are also actively shaping history. So now I ask: What history will you write?

Afterword

This story serves as a tribute to the heroes of history, individuals from all walks of life who shaped a country even without knowing that their actions would have enduring effects throughout time.

To you, thank you. Thank you for joining me on this journey and for recognizing the human spirit within the pages of history. If these stories resonated with you or sparked curiosity, I would be delighted to hear from you. Your voice holds significance, and sharing your thoughts by leaving a genuine review could be a small yet meaningful way to connect with others. To do that, you only need to Click Here.

With gratitude and optimism for a future where each one of us contributes to the ongoing narrative.

Razin Lewis

www.ingramcontent.com/pod-product-compliance
Lightning Source LLC
Chambersburg PA
CBHW071733150726
47998CB00005B/1618